BILL ODDIE'S
Little
Black Bird Book

BILL ODDIE'S
Little
Black Bird Book

EYRE METHUEN   LONDON

First published in 1980 by
Eyre Methuen Ltd
11 New Fetter Lane, London EC4P 4EE

Oddie, Bill
 Bill Oddie's little black bird book.
 1. Bird watching – Great Britain – Anecdotes,
 facetiae, satire, etc.
 I. Little black bird book
 598.2′073′0941   QL690.G7

 ISBN 0–413–47820–3

Printed in Great Britain by
Butler & Tanner Ltd, Frome and London

Contents

List of illustrations

This is one of the very few books about birds that does not begin with a Foreword by Robert Dougal.

Or HRH Prince Philip.

Or Prince Charles.

Or any other Royal Person.

Or Humphrey Lyttleton.

Or Eric Morecambe.

Or Billy Fury.

Or anyone else famous with a supposed interest in bird-watching.[1]

This is *Bill Oddie's Little Black Bird Book*. The information in this book is true, really and honestly true, which makes it even more scurrilous. The publishers disown it. If you consider it libellous you don't sue Eyre Methuen. You sue Bill Oddie. He wrote the book – got that? – BILL ODDIE is the author.

[1] Having read the proofs, all of them refused to have anything to do with it (Publisher).[2]

[2] Which is OK by me (Author).

About the author

(BY SOMEBODY WHO KNOWS HIM QUITE
WELL, AND THEREFORE WISHES TO REMAIN
ANONYMOUS)

Bill Oddie is the only proper 'show-biz' bird person. There
are lots of show-biz people who *say* they are 'into birds'.
Under the heading of show-biz I would include sporting
people, politicians, news readers and, of course, royalty – well
they make *me* laugh (and if dressing up in purple cloaks and
wearing jewels and funny hats isn't 'show-biz', what is?).
But *none* of them really get out there and *do it*. I mean, when
was the last time you saw Prince Philip sneaking through a
hole in the fence at Reading sewage farm? Does Robert
Dougal *really* know how to separate the Asiatic and American races of Lesser Golden Plover? Is there *anything* in Billy
Fury's singing that indicates that he has been even slightly
influenced by hearing the flight-call of a Little Bunting? Oh,
I have no doubt all of them own a pair of binoculars, regularly put out bags of peanuts, and are fully paid up members
of the RSPB. But have they ever even *been* to Minsmere –
except perhaps for a guided tour of the Marsh Harriers,
greeted no doubt by a guard of honour of sixty avocets? I
mean, I bet none of *them* have crawled under a gate on all
fours before dawn and been chased off by six armed wardens
on a tractor. Well Bill Oddie has![1]

[1] Author: It *was* a long time ago (well *quite* a long time ago).

Of course I do not by any means wish to disparage the interest in and support of our feathered friends shown by other show-biz personalities, but, own up, only Bill Oddie knows the bird world as it *really* is. The tension, the scandal, and the shame. No, he may not be as famous as that lot as a show-biz personality, but he is definitely *more* famous as a bird-watcher.[2, 3] So this book is about bird-watchers and bird-watching, and occasionally about birds, and Bill Oddie is highly qualified to write it. This is true. If you still don't believe me, a full list of his qualifications appears on the next page.

[2] Infamous (Editor).
[3] Actually I consider myself to be nearly as famous as Robert Dougal, and much younger, though with a less pleasant speaking voice. I admit, I am *not* as famous as Prince Philip, and I am also smaller, but I do have a lot more hair. I am not as famous or as funny as Eric Morecambe, but I am a better bird-watcher. Come to think of it, there are lots of bird-watchers who are much funnier than me, and they are also better bird-watchers; but they are not as famous as I am. Whilst we are at it, I also greatly admire Buster Keaton and Tom[4] and Jerry, but they have no connection at all with birds – except that I assume Tom eats them (Author).
[4] Tom has also made several short cartoons with Tweetie Pie (Editor).[5]
[5] Tweetie Pie is a mule canary not a wild bird, and therefore doesn't count (Author).

Bill Oddie's qualifications

May 1947: Found an egg in a nest, put it in a match box; put match box in pocket and sat on it. The next day – identified the bits of egg shell – hedge sparrow.

1947–54: Continued to pinch birds' eggs discreetly and unforgivably, but at least he became an expert on identifying the species which had laid them. Nowadays he'd have been quite rightly fined or possibly locked up.

Still in juvenile plumage.

Note the tendency to exhibitionism even at an early age.

Bill at Fair Isle, late 1950s

Bartley Reservoir

Note the bloodstained spikes which kept bird-watchers away from the birds.

Also note the absence of birds.

1954: Gave up egg collecting and *instantly* became a better person. Began regular bird watching visits to Bartley Reservoir – a nasty bleak concrete-shored stretch of water near Birmingham, which was occasionally also visited by birds.

1956: First birding holidays to the Exe estuary in Devon, Portland Bill and Cley in Norfolk. The experience was written up in his first permanent notebook and constitutes the earliest visible evidence that Bill Oddie had become a bird watcher. Since then he has kept full documentation of all hours spent watching birds and this runs to twelve volumes of big hardback exercise books. During these early years he lived in Birmingham, where he also went to school. He went to university in Cambridge, and watched birds all over the place. Here is some proof of his experience:

1956–64: Countless visits to Bartley reservoir. Eventually published a paper for the West Midland Bird Club on the 'Birds of Bartley Reservoir'. Also regular trips round other Midland reservoirs and bird spots. As secretary of the Natural History Society at King Edward's School, Birmingham, Bill organised an elaborate study of the birds of Edgbaston Park.

Edgbaston Pool

With lots of birds hiding in the reeds — honest!

Early sixties, moved to Hagley, Worcestershire, and concentrated bird visits on Upton Warren pools, which is now a nationally-known reserve.

1956–64: Many holidays at bird observatories including Cley, Norfolk (many times), Bradwell (Essex), Dungeness

Upton Warren

Before they built lots of hides and scared the birds away.

This is NOT the actual observatory - its just where they kept the kids. Grown-up bird watchers were allowed to stay in the nice comfy old house in the background.

First birding holiday, Monk's House

(Kent), Spey Valley (Scotland) and Fair Isle in the Shetlands. During several visits to Monk's House Bird Observatory and the Farne Islands in Northumberland he gained extensive experience in trapping and ringing birds and became a qualified ringer.

1965: Moved permanently to London where he still lives. Since then to the present day his so-called 'work' – doing silly radio and TV programmes and making idiotic records – has prevented him from really intensive regular study of a local area. He does still get about a bit round London, Sussex and Kent, but most of his watching is done on bird holidays. Here is a list to prove it:

1965 Minsmere and Cley
1966 Southern Portugal and Cley
1967 Hauxley and Cley
1968 The Solway, Minorca and Cornwall
1969 Southern Ireland and Scilly
1970 Fair Isle and Minsmere

Moulting into
Adult Plumage

At the Scillies, mid 1960s

1971 Southern Ireland, New York, Majorca and Southern Ireland again
1972 Scilly and Tunisia
1973 Cape Cod (USA), Portland and Scilly
1974 Portland, Cley, Scilly and Cornwall
1975 Out Skerries, Shetland, Scilly and Portland
1976 Sutherland, Out Skerries, Canada, Fair Isle and Scilly
1977 Cley, New York and Portland
1978 Queensland (Australia), Scilly, Out Skerries, Scilly and Scilly again
1979 India, Scilly, Fair Isle, Crete, Southern Ireland and Portland
1980 Thailand, Scilly and Fair Isle

A fuller account of these travels may be found in his second book. But read this one first, please, because the second one isn't published yet. Mainly because he hasn't written it. Bill Oddie is President of Sandwich Bay Bird Observatory and a Council member of the Royal Society for the Protection of Birds.

Out Skerries

A nasty place – you wouldn't
like it here – just leave it to me ... please!

Bill in India, 1979

Full adult plumage.
Note shoulder-bag full of curry.

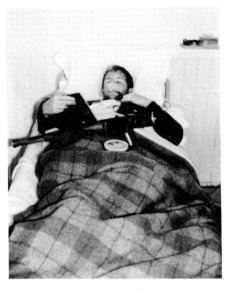

Deciding which rare bird he's going to go out and pretend to see when it stops raining.

A wet day on Fair Isle

Bill has recently taken to trying to draw and paint birds. He hasn't been doing it very long, so he has some excuse for not being very good at it. He occasionally takes very bad photographs and is unlikely to improve.

He has seen 325 species in Britain, which isn't very impressive considering that he is already 38 years old; *but* he is quite good at recognising them.

The rest of the book is written by me (Bill Oddie) OK. So here goes ...

The author's foreword

(BY BILL ODDIE AND *NOT* THE FRIEND WHO KNOWS HIM VERY WELL)

What is a bird-watcher? Non-bird-watchers tend to have a certain image of what bird-watchers are like. They are little unmarried ladies in tweed suits, with long woolly stockings, curly walking-sticks and a pair of binoculars that look like opera glasses.

If they are *not* little old ladies, they are retired colonels, still in tweed suits, woolly stockings etc, but with the addition of a deer stalker hat and a moustache. If they are neither little old ladies or little old colonels, then they are sensitive 'loners'. Middle-aged men (or even young men) quietly dedicated; with that mysterious 'inner peace' that comes from living in close harmony with nature. They wear white fishermen's polo-necked sweaters, live in old windmills near marshes, and spend a lot of time gazing into windswept skies listening for the cry of the wild geese returning from the 'north'. So – bird-watcher – quaint and cranky? Or rugged and mystical? But either way, all of them are surely united by a common feeling, a shared sensitivity, a mutual love . . . the mystery and magic of birds.

Do me a favour!

Bird-watchers are tense, competitive, selfish, shifty, dishonest, distrusting, boorish, arrogant, pedantic, unsentimental and above all envious. OK, not *all* of them are *all* of those

things, although I know several that *are*. But most of them
are at least two or three. I personally am four or five, depending on my mood. And some days I am nine or ten. I've got
several other objectionable qualities, all directly attributable
to my obsession with birds. I admit I also know many bird-
watchers who are affable, generous, witty and delightful
company – but *they're* no fun. And anyway, even *they* aren't
perfect.

The fact is, birds bring out the worst in people. And, what's
more, bird-watching probably attracts a greater number of
'loonies' than any other hobby; and of a greater variety, from
'upper-class twits' to punks. The proof is in this book. So
why then the fallacious public image of the bird-watcher?
Simply because so many so-called 'bird books' are written
by people who know bugger all about birds! Their ignorance
allows them to indulge a level of sentimentality which simply
isn't borne out by the facts. I mean, no half-serious bird-
watcher could enjoy (let alone write!) a book called, with
offensive imprecision, *Jonathan Livingston-Seagull* For a start,
assuming you *want* to get all cosmic and allegorical about
bird's wondrous power of flight – would you *honestly* choose
a bleedin' gull!? They spend most of their time scrabbling
around on rubbish tips! They are ugly, and quarrelsome, and
they pollute drinking water on reservoirs. And anyway
Jonathan Livingston-*what* gull. I *know* it looks very classy
floating around silhouetted against the evening sun – but that
only makes it harder to identify. And the fact is that in the
film the continuity of plumage phases was totally to cock;
and they turned it into a completely different species in one
scene! No. I'm sorry but I'm not prepared to be impressed
by intimations of immortality from an author who shows
such scant regard for the real world. Any spirituality worth
meditation time, has to be based on *truth*. And *truth is fact*.
(And 'seagull' isn't *fact*, it's a cop out.) I'm sorry to wax all
philosophical, but that's how I feel. You write me *Jonathan*

Livingston-Second Winter Lesser Black-backed Gull and I might get off on it.

You see – I've got all aggressive now – opinionated, intolerant. Two more objectionable qualities – no, three (if you include 'aggressive') to add to my list. I said I'd prove it – birds *do* bring out the worst in people.

Well now, maybe you don't want the worst brought out in *you*, and maybe you are a non-bird-watcher thinking of taking it up – and more and more people are taking it up – in fact there's too flippin' many of them (there's some parts of the country where you can't see the birds for the bird-watchers) – well, if this book puts you off the whole idea, so much the better.

And if you already are a bird-watcher perhaps you'll be struck by a suitable sense of shame, and pack it in. But I doubt it. Bird-watching is an obsession, a disease even, and if you've got it you won't get rid of it. What the author of *Jonathan Livingston–Seagull* doesn't understand is that you don't need to search for any pseudo-mystical religion by staring at the 'seagulls' ... identify the gull properly – and you've *found* your religion. Get it? Bird-watching *is* the religion. Of course, any bird-watcher knows this. You *know* how strongly you care; how deeply you feel. Sometimes it almost *hurts* – but do you know *why*? Read on ...

1
Why watch birds?

WHAT MAKES A BIRD-WATCHER TICK?

The emotion a bird-watcher knows best is jealousy – the most insidious and powerful of the deadly sins! Why? Because bird-watching is collecting. Just as a stamp-collector collects stamps, or a train-spotter collects train-numbers, a bird watcher collects birds, and ulcers. So let's follow the analogy. If a stamp-collector does not own a penny black he is jealous of the collector who does. The lucky owner of a Guyanan 'Octagonal' enjoys a sensation of almost euphoric smugness because no other stamp-collector has got one – and all the rest are jealous of him. The aim of the train-spotter is to have more train numbers in his little book than any other train-spotter, and anyone else who has more is a rival. Well, it's just the same with birds. A bird-watcher 'collects' birds; and some bird-watchers have collected an awful lot, others very few indeed.

How do you collect birds? Not literally 'dead or alive'. (Some people *do*; but they are called either hunters or cage-bird specialist – aviculturalists or something – not bird watchers.) No, the bird-watcher 'collects' a bird by identifying it. Quite simply, if he sees something and he can put a name to it he can say he is collecting that species. That's one he can 'tick off' in his book, and he can keep a list of species he's seen. So, instantly we have grounds for comparison, competitiveness and jealousy. As for *any* collector, the thrilling anticipation of adding another item to your collection is an emotional strain. It is even more of a strain if you fail to add it. And it's a *hell* of a strain if somebody else adds it and you don't.

OK, these little stresses and disappointments can occur to stamp-collectors and train-spotters, but at least they are controllable or even predictable. If you pay enough to the right dealer you will add a rare stamp to your collection, and if you are outbid somebody else will own it; it's tough and it's galling, but it's sort of under human control. A train-spotter by and large only has to be able to read a time-table, and keep up a touching faith in the efficiency of British Rail, and he can eventually tick off every train on the rails. Trains might be late, might be cancelled, might even crash, but they don't just disappear never to be seen again. But birds do – they fly away! Just as you are about to identify one – and definitely something new for your list – it flies away, never to be seen again – not by *you* anyway.

Worse still, it lands right in front of another bird-watcher, and allows *him* to identify and add it to *his* list; and that evening *he'll* tell *you* about it. But when you go back next morning, it's flown away again. And if it's a *really* rare bird, you may *never* see one again for the rest of your life!

All this conspires to make the collecting of birds continually fraught with tension. It's no wonder that many bird-watchers try very hard indeed not to make lists at all, and certainly to kid themselves that they don't really care about how long their list is, or how long anybody else's list is. But it's a losing battle – *all* bird-watchers keep lists; even if it's only a list of how many times they've claimed they don't keep a list! And, of course, like the stamp-collector who craves for his penny black, the bird-watcher craves to see a rare bird.

So what constitutes a 'rare' bird? Well, of course, this is comparative. For a kick off, anything that isn't actually on your list can be considered, in a sense, rare – at least it's new to *you* and that's the most important thing. On the other hand, to a complete beginner a Chaffinch might be new,

This is a female Chaffinch. To be honest without any colour it could be a male Chaffinch. But its meant to be a female. The publishers cant afford to show you a male; but at least it means this book is fairly cheap. Mind you, so it should be.

whilst a more experienced bird-watcher might well mock it. Quite literally. I have certainly seen experienced bird-watchers mocking chaffinches. I've done it myself, I admit.

'Gosh what's that?' yells the excited beginner.

'It's only a bleedin' chaffinch,' I have mocked, 'it's *only* the commonest bird in Britain isn't it!? Huh.'

With experience, time and arrogance, the bird-watcher accepts that 'rarity' is defined more geographically. So a 'rare bird' may be a bird never before or only rarely recorded, say, in the county. Or even rarer, and preferable, a bird only rarely recorded in Britain. The most sought after being something *never* before recorded in Britain – 'A first for Britain.'

Well, more of that later. For the moment, let's accept that all bird-watchers do enjoy seeing rare birds, and new birds, and do enjoy adding birds to their lists. They won't all admit it mind you, but the fact is that it's *always* possible to make a bird-watcher jealous. Just tell them you've seen a species they've always wanted to see and they'll have a few pangs! All of them. They'll try to be magnanimous perhaps.

'Oh great,' (note the gritted teeth) 'Is it still there?'

'Nope, flown away.'

'Oh never mind, er ... what was it like? Was it easy to identify?'

'Oh yes fairly, it had white wing-bars, big eye stripe and ...'

'Yes ... well I'm sure I'll see one *some day*. Something else to look forward to. GRRRR.'

That question about 'was it easy to identify', *that's* significant. It raises just a glimmer of hope that the other fellow *might* have made a mistake. At worst, there's an ungracious tendency among some bird-watchers towards an attitude of 'If *I* didn't see it, I don't believe it'. But, let's face it, this time, *he's* seen a species you haven't seen, and *his* list has got longer, and yours hasn't – *and* the lousy little bird has flown away! And yes, you *do* care.

All bird watchers make lists – whether in their heads or in their notebooks – and the competitiveness of list keeping is a tension-maker. Even if you are only competing with your own list – it's always there, potentially longer than it is at present – a challenge. But fortunately, lists can also let you off the hook of constant comparison. Maybe you are a casual weekend bird-watcher. Maybe you rarely get away from your own garden. You are *never* going to be able to compete with the manic bird-watcher racing round the country chasing every rarity he hears about. Don't despair.

You can still enjoy the thrills, excitement and achievement simply by *limiting* your list to, say, 'Birds I have seen in my garden'. Mind you, your nextdoor neighbour may have still seen more than you. If so, don't build a higher fence. Redefine the list to 'Birds I have seen from my bedroom window', and then it's odds on your list is going to be longer than anybody else's. Unless you are having a scene with a lady birdwatcher – and, actually, if her list is longer than yours, then I should pack it in as a bad job (the scene not the list).

As with many aspects of birding, the enjoyment and the heartbreak are inextricably mixed. List-making undoubtedly causes tension, but it can also relieve it. Most important of all, it can create the excitement and challenge that is essential to satisfactory 'collecting'. This is serious and practical advice. Keep a list, lots of lists, and you'll never be bored. Here is a list of lists you can keep (it will be familiar to all birders):

A life list (birds you've seen anywhere in the world ever).
A British list (birds you've seen in Britain)
A county list (birds you've seen in your home county)
A local reservoir list (birds you've seen on your regular patch)
A garden list (birds you've seen in your own garden)
A year list (birds you've seen this year)
A month list (birds you've seen this month)
A day list (birds you've seen today)
A 'now' list (birds visible now)
A trip list (birds you see on your holiday)
A journey list (birds you see from the train or the car to or from your holiday) etc. etc.

You will make your lists and you will use them, and find in them motivation and consolation. But there is one final list no birder can push too far into the back of his mind, and it is the list that keeps you at it – 'Birds I haven't seen yet'.

2
What am I? What are you?

So far I have rather indiscriminately used the terms 'bird-watcher' and 'birder' as if they were interchangeable. This is not really the case. There are several words that loosely denote that a person is into birds. The truth is, each of them has a special connotation; usually an implication of serious-ness and competence. And there's a sort of hobby-snobbery involved. To revive a previous analogy – a more serious stamp-collector calls himself a philatelist; and, even more outrageously, a person heavily into trains is not a train-spotter but a ferro-equinologist (an iron-horsist, no less). It isn't just playing with words. One presumes the philatelist knows something about where the stamps come from, their ages, their water-marks, their little perforations etc. The stamp-collector just sticks them in an album and doesn't even always use the proper hinges. It's the same in the bird world, but with an insidious range of nuances. Let's assume you want to develop your interest in birds and you want to know what to call yourself. What title will command the most respect and indicate that you pursue your hobby (or rather obsession) with appropriate degrees of seriousness and expertise? This is quite tricky, and quite complicated, so you will have to concentrate; and you'll eventually have a delicate decision to make. If you call yourself by the wrong title you'll arouse all sorts of expectations which may embarrass you. Let's start with the intellectual one, the big word, the bird equivalent of ferro-equinologist ...

Ornithologist

This is a very dangerous one. It implies a high level of expertise of a scientific nature. Unless you have a biology or zoology degree, or are an expert on some particular obscure area of bird behaviour, don't claim to be an ornithologist. I have been accused of being an ornithologist (by laymen who wished to be impressed, or journalists who wish to impress their readers) and I always strenuously deny it. Neither do I believe I know any bird person who would call themselves an ornithologist.

As I have explained, one of the principal motivations of birding is collecting and list making, or to put it rather more nicely *identifying species*. This is *not* the obsession of an ornithologist. Being a scientist he is above such things and can perhaps rightfully claim a moral superiority. If you are confident or smug enough to want to claim moral superiority, good luck to you. And if you really *are* morally superior, then you have my admiration, and no place in this book.

A facile definition might be that the *normal* bird-person is interested in what the bird *is*, whilst the ornithologist is interested in what it *does*. Or, to add a little biological implication, the *normal* bird person is concerned exclusively with the *outside* of the bird – i.e. what it looks like – whilst the ornithologist is often concerned with the *inside* – they may well cut them up, examine them, etc.

If you are still not clear about it – chances are, you are not an ornithologist.

Ornithologist is, however, the only title that is too *serious*. Nearly all the others are too *frivolous*. Unless you want to avoid being drawn into heavy discussion (perhaps you've only just started and don't want to show yourself up) or unless you want to get a cheap laugh, you *do not* call yourself either a

Bird-spotter or a bird-fancier

A bird-fancier is either more appropriately applicable to a person who keeps caged birds, or it is a pathetic joke made by some bore in a pub who has just heard that you are interested in birds.

'Oh. Ho-ho, *I'm* a bit of a bird-fancier too, eh? eh!'

I'll tell you how to deal with *him* later in the book (something to look forward to, eh?). For now, just ignore it (actually that's one way to deal with him).

You can be more easily forgiven for calling yourself a bird-spotter, but don't – because it's soppy. It's particularly soppy if you say you're 'going bird-spotting'. Say it out loud a few times and you'll see what I mean:

'Bird-spotting.'

'I'm going spotting birds.'

'Oh look! I've spotted a bird.'

'See that bird? I just spotted it. That is now a having-been-spotted bird.'

'I'm now a bird-spotter – spot, spot, spot I go.'

See, it *is* a silly word. It conjures up pictures of people hiding and peeping round bushes and popping up and down. It always reminds me of those daft little line drawings in old Baden Powell books with names like *Scouting for Boys*. And I wouldn't go scouting for boys any more than I'd go bird-spotting.

Of course it's up to you. Call yourself a bird-spotter if you want to. But don't be surprised if people giggle at you, especially other bird persons. OK, I shall keep you in suspense no longer – so what *should* you call yourself?

EARNING YOUR BIRD-SPOTTERS BADGE

Bird-watcher

No! Now this is a surprise isn't it?! So what's *wrong* with bird-watcher? I don't know. I honestly don't know, *but* it is *not* the correct term. Not any more.

A few years ago, it used to be fine – an accurate descriptive title. A bird-watcher watched birds, and not only that, he or she knew what they were watching, and it was a serious interest, but not esoteric. So why not bird-watcher any more? I can only think it's because bird-watching became so popular that new gradations of snobbery were required. A few years ago a bird-watcher was a fairly unique title, but nowadays there are an *awful* lot of them. It just isn't *exclusive* enough. Anyone who has taken some time out of life to develop a little expertise likes to feel they have qualified for membership of some kind of élite. There may be something like a million people in this country who would confidently claim to be bird-watchers, and that's too many to constitute an élite. So – here goes – the correct word is...

Birder

A birder is seriously involved in studying, identifying and collecting birds. He or she goes *watching birds*, but on the other hand he or she *doesn't* go *bird-watching* – he goes 'birding'. This implies a fair degree of conviction and expertise. Moreover – and I think this may explain some of the word's appeal – it implies a certain ruggedness, almost athleticism. Bird-watching does sound a bit *passive*. Like you sit quietly and hope the bird will fly to you, and if it does, you watch it. Birding is more active. You definitely *move*, quite quickly if necessary; and if the birds don't show themselves, you get out there and find them. Track them down, and flush them out. And you don't just *watch* them, you *study* them, *identify* them, and move on to the next lot. Here's excitement, here's dedication ... here's birding. Not bird-watching, or spotting or fancying – *birding*. Got it?

So ... Have you decided? Are you a 'birder', the real thing, or are you just a 'dude'?
     A what?
     I said, a dude.
     Isn't that something out of a cowboy film?
     No, it's a term used by twitchers.
     By what?
     By twitchers.
     What is a twitcher?
     Well, a twitcher is a particular kind of birder.
     But didn't you just say that birder was the right name?
     Indeed I did. A twitcher *is* a birder. But a birder isn't necessarily a twitcher, and a bird-watcher needn't really be a dude, though a lot of them are – according to twitchers.
     OK now you are *really* confused perchance. I shall explain ... It is very important that you know exactly what you are, and what everyone else is in the 'bird world'. Because not

all bird persons are unified by single enthusiasm. Some of them simply do not get on with one another, and you might have to take sides. So, let us define...

Twitcher

You will recall (I hope) all that stuff about seeing new birds and rare birds and ticking them off on your list. Right, well a twitcher is a birder who races round the country frantically collecting rare birds. He is openly concerned with adding more and more species to his list. His obsession is to get a new tick. Basically there is nothing wrong with this, and most birders would admit that there is a little bit of twitcher in all of us. What distinguishes the *real* twitcher is his degree of emotional involvement in whether or not he succeeds in getting a new tick. Hence the supposed origin of the name. If this kind of birder gets to hear that a bird has been sighted that would be a tick for him, he is so wracked with nervous anticipation (that he might see it) or trepidation (that he might miss it) that he literally twitches with the excitement of it all. If he then fails to see the bird, naturally he twitches even more in his anguish of disappointment. This may seem an exaggeration of the emotions involved, but it is hardly so. I have certainly seen twitchers twitch, shake, and even throw up under stress.

Perhaps some of the depth of involvement is conveyed by the words of a young twitcher, who told me: 'If I know that there is a new bird around, nothing will stop me seeing it – nothing!' To a guy with such a philosophy distance and danger are no barriers. Twitchers frequently cover vast distances in their pursuit of rare birds.

News of a rare bird spreads along what is called the grapevine – a sort of jungle telegraph that is as mysterious as it is efficient. No one quite knows how it works – and I personally have suspected telepathy. For example, in September 1979

Yellow-billed Cuckoo, cowering from the gaze
of 300 twitchers and a hungry kestrel.
Note how the bird is obligingly hiding it,
feet so that I dont have to try and draw
them. Most bird-artists find feet very difficult –
I find them impossible.
The lower part of the bill is ,actually, yellow!
This one was stained greeny from caterpillar blood.

while I was filming a TV show near Portland Bill Bird
Observatory (a location chosen quite coincidentally by the
BBC, with absolutely no pressure from me), I was lucky
enough to find a Yellow-billed Cuckoo (a rare visitor from
America). The bird was rather elusive, but by the evening
about four or five birders from the observatory had also
managed to see it. Announcement of its arrival was not actually broadcast on Nationwide – indeed no effort was made
to spread the news, as the bird was on private farmland.
Nevertheless, by dawn next morning there were two
hundred twitchers lined up along the side of the field waiting
for the bird to reappear – which, being a yankee exhibitionist,

it did. That's how efficient the grapevine is. And such is the attraction of a rare bird that by the end of the cuckoo's four or five day stay, it was estimated that at least a thousand twitchers had ticked it off. And yet perhaps even more mysterious is the way the negative grapevine works equally efficiently. On the Friday afternoon, the cuckoo was seen being eyed by a hungry-looking kestrel. At one point the kestrel actually grabbed it and carried it off, only to be pursued by a gang of anxious twitchers, who so moved the falcon with their howls of dismay that it dropped the rarity immediately. Not surprisingly, however, the cuckoo decided to quit Dorset that evening. Saturday's sun dawned on two or three hundred twitchers, who, by ten o'clock, were close to tears as they had to accept that their quarry had either flown or literally been scared to death by the kestrel. Still sad, but undaunted, they leapt back into their cars, onto their bikes or set off hitching to the next available tick; some to Cornwall, some to Norfolk. The reverse grapevine spread the news that the cuckoo had gone so efficiently that no twitcher visited Portland after lunch, and the next morning there were no twitchers by the field where the cuckoo had been. Which was ironical, for as it turned out, several rare birds turned up at Portland that weekend which would no doubt have been ticks for many of the itinerant birders.

Which brings us to a fairly crucial part of the twitcher's philosophy. Whilst to many birders the major thrill is to actually find a new or rare bird for themselves, the twitcher is more frequently to be found in pursuit of *other people's* birds. Whilst birding may be assumed to be a relatively solitary activity, it is not so for twitchers. Usually they hunt in packs.

Let's say it's Friday evening. The grapevine has spread the news of this weekend's available ticks, so all over the country groups of twitchers plan their weekend itinerary. The birds are pin-pointed on the map, and away the twitchers go; the distances travelled are truly phenomenal.

Here's a map showing a possible weekend's twitching itinerary — and whilst I'm at it I've marked in a few of the country's "good spots"... rather a lot aren't there!? During October there's probably good birds at many of these places, so the choice is agony! And there's hundreds of other places I haven't marked.

Shetland ***
FAIR ISLE *****
Orkney *

Start FRIDAY NIGHT & back for work on MONDAY MORNING.
Route:
Birmingham to Hauxley to Shotton to Holme Swanscombe to Stodmarsh to Tamar Lake (and possibly Cornwall) and back to Birmingham.
N.B. Not all twitchers come from Birmingham.

Best routes are available from the Automobile Association. Train fare lists and timetables from British Rail. Air travel details from British Airways, or private charter firms. Bikes from Curry's Or you may prefer to hitch-hike — or forget the whole idea.
AND THERE'S LOTS OF "UNDISCOVERED" PLACES IN IRELAND ....

AKEAGH LOCH ***

BALLYCOTTON ***
CAPE CLEAR ***

LISSAGRIFFIN ** LAKE

TACUMSHIN AND LADY'S ISLAND *

WEXFORD SLOBS **

SCOTLAND
Land of mystery — usually overlooked on the way to Fair Isle... o

Isle of May *
A.M. SATURDAY
Holy Island
Hauxley
Solway
Tyne-side + Tees-side + The Humber
the Ribble
NORTH BULL *
Anglesey
Calf of Man
Shotton SATURDAY P.M.
Bardsey o
Skokholm
WALES (not a lot here).
Lavernock
Blackpill *
Lundy **
Porlock
Hayle
Chew Valley
Staffs Reservoirs
Wisbech Ouse
BIRMINGHAM Wales
FRIDAY NIGHT
Slimbridge
London Reservoirs
Exe
Radipole
PORTLAND
St Catherines Pt.
Tamar Lake
Cornwall
SUNDAY NEARLY DARK
Porth gwarra
SCILLY *****
SUNDAY P.M. OPTIONAL - miss out SHOTTON?
possibly

Spurn * o Gibraltar Point *
Holme
SATURDAY EVENING
Wells & Holkham
SUNDAY A.M.
CLEY ****
Minsmere ***
Walberswick
the Naze
Abberton
Swanscombe
SANDWICH **
Stodmarsh SUNDAY P.M.
DUNGENESS ***
Farlington Pagham Stanpit
Rye
Beachy Head **

This fictitious weekend twitching schedule is by no means fantasy:

Set out from Birmingham, Friday evening – drive all night to Northumberland. Saturday morning, tick off Pallas's Warbler at Hauxley. Drive across to Cheshire Dee to tick off Wilson's Phalarope at Shotton Pools. Drive in the afternoon across to Holme in Norfolk to tick off Dusky Warbler on Saturday evening. (If it's too dark tick it off first thing on Sunday morning.) Drive via Swanscombe (for Lesser Yellow Legs) to Stodmarsh for possible Blue-winged Teal and late Purple Heron. Then drive over to Tamar Lake on Devon/Cornwall border for Baird's Sandpiper or optionally, try for Lesser Golden Plover or Lesser Kestrel both reported somewhere in Cornwall.

Sleep and comfort are not important. There may be five or six twitchers in one Mini. They will take it in turns to drive and sleep. When they arrive at the bird, they will expect to find a small crowd of maybe two hundred or so twitchers. If their information has not accurately pin-pointed exactly which bush the rare bird was last seen in, it doesn't matter – you just follow the crowd. The fact that the bird is already being watched by two hundred people means you don't have to waste any time identifying it for yourself. So an efficient twitch simply goes:

'Where is it?'

'Over there.'

'Oh yes.... Great. (Tick) Tarra...' and on to the next one...

From Birmingham to Northumberland to Norfolk to Kent to Devon and back. Well now, even with six of you sharing the petrol costs, covering several hundred miles every weekend will set you back a bit. The dedicated twitcher works and saves, and all available funds are spent in the pursuit of birds. In many cases, work becomes merely a means of earning money so that you can afford to keep twitching.

The most enterprising example I know is a group of young

Three hundred twitchers at Falmouth in March 1980,
having a Forster's Tern.

twitchers who settled themselves for a year or so up in the Shetland Isles (itself an excellent bird area). These lads worked on the building sites and installations which have proliferated in Shetland with the development of North Sea oil. They earned a fair wack by putting in a lot of overtime, but they lived cheaply, ate simply and dressed roughly. All the money was put aside so they could afford to chase the many rare birds that turn up in the northern isles. And you do need money to chase birds round Shetland, since rarities drop down on the scattered islands, and the only way to be on the spot quickly is to charter a small plane, which is not cheap! If you are based in Shetland, it means you are also within twitching distance of Fair Isle Bird Observatory, which can boast more 'firsts for Britain' than any other locality. So, especially during the peak migration periods of spring and autumn, the Shetland-based twitching group would ring up the observatory first thing in the morning (and sometimes a bit too early for the warden's comfort) with the key question: 'Anything about?' If the answer was 'No', the twitchers put in another day's work and stashed the loot aside for the happy moment when the answer was 'Yes. We've got a Cretzchmar's Bunting, Spectacled Warbler,' or whatever rare bird had graced Fair Isle with its presence. In this case, work was dropped for the day. This group seemed to have developed a working (or non-working) understanding with their foreman, whom I presume accepted that their wayward attendance would be compensated for by extra hours and effort when there weren't any rare birds around. The group then raced down to the airport at Sumburgh and piled into one of the small planes run by Loganair Company which serves the various islands. By air, Fair Isle becomes a fifteen minute hop from Sumburgh (it's three and a half sickening hours by the little boat, which only goes twice a week anyway). So, not much over an hour after hearing of a rarity on Fair Isle, these lads could be seeing it and ticking it, and

if the twitch was efficient and quick, they could be back at
work for the afternoon shift. Even with a full consignment
– six or seven people – plane-chartering is not a frugal way
to travel, and I've known the same group charter the plane
two or three times within the week – and, incidently, fail
to see any of the birds they were chasing!

Nor would that particular group confine themselves to
such local hops as Fair Isle or the various Shetland Isles. If

Spectacled Warbler ♂
Clinging to a cliff-face on Fair Isle
when it should've been in a bush
in the South of France.
It says in the books this species
is "volatile" which means it leaps
about a lot ... which it did.

a rare bird was reported from more or less any other part
of Britain, they could afford both the time off and the money
to go to see it, if it was considered a good enough tick. And
to add further to the expense and mileage, it would be more
or less unthinkable not to spend at least part of October down
in the Scilly Isles, which is about as far as you can get from
Shetland whilst still remaining in Britain.

Probably October is the best month for rare birds in Britain, and it is especially during October that there is a triangu-

lar phone connection which more or less spans the country.
The three points of the triangle are Fair Isle (and hence Shetland, the specific phoning point being the bird observatory),
Cley in Norfolk (the phone in use here used to be in the
George Hotel) and the Scilly Isles (the Mermaid Inn or the
Atlantic Hotel bar on the island of St Mary's). During
October a fair percentage of Britain's twitchers will be based
at one or other of these three localities. And on any evening
in October news of rare birds travels the wires between these
three points (the day time is spent seeing the birds). The Nor-
folk-based twitcher is, in a way, best positioned, as he is more
or less equidistant between the north and the south. So if he
makes a dash for Fair Isle or Scilly he only has about five
hundred miles to travel either way. On the other hand, fewer
real rarities turn up actually *in* Norfolk. It is certainly not
unknown for Shetland and Scilly twitchers to do a quick
thousand-mile exchange trip. So Shetland twitchers can nip
down and tick off the latest Scilly rarity, whilst the Scilly
twitchers belt up to Fair Isle. I'm not sure what the actual
record travelling time is, but just for interest and in case you
are thinking of testing it, as far as I can figure out the most
efficient schedule for from Fair Isle to Scilly would be . . .

Leave Fair Isle, Loganair chartered flight at 16.00 hours
Arrive Sumburgh at 16.15 hours
Leave Sumburgh, British Airways scheduled flight at 16.50
hours
Arrive Aberdeen at 17.15 hours
Leave Aberdeen at 20.55 hours
Arrive London, Heathrow at 22.15 hours
Taxi or Underground train into central London
Leave London Paddington on British Rail Sleeper train
00.10 hours
Arrive Penzance 08.00 hours
Airport bus to Heliport

Leave Penzance British Airways helicopter at 08.50 hours
Arrive St Mary's, Scilly 09.10 hours
Taxi to St Mary's quay, to catch small regular boat leaving
St Mary's at 10.15 hours
Arrive St Agnes 10.40 hours and be ticking the rarities
before 11 o'clock.

This way you can have left Fair Isle in the late afternoon and
have arrived in Scilly by early the next morning. You have
only lost four hours of daylight birding time. Mind you, its
cost you about £200!

High-powered twitching involves money, travelling,
dedication and enterprise. The point was rather neatly
proved to me in February 1980. I and a group of birder
friends were watching exotic species halfway up a mountain
in northern Thailand. A dusty car screeched to a halt and that
familiar emotive question rang through the Asian morning
in clear anxious English tones: 'Anything about?' I turned
to see five young English twitchers tumbling out of the car
– the Shetland group! I had last met them the previous June
on Fair Isle, on that occasion tumbling out of a plane in a

Cretzchmar's Bunting. ♂

Cowering on Fair Isle, & deciding to
fly away before it gets twitched.

Chestnut Thrush
– a "first" for Thailand – as far as we know.

frantic and unsuccessful search for a Cretzchmar's Bunting (only the second ever recorded in Britain). Had the news that we had seen a Chestnut Thrush the previous day (a new species to Thailand no less) been passed down the grapevine and already reached Shetland? Had they left the building site and chartered a Concorde just to see our Thrush? Now *that's* what I call twitching! The real answer was of course even more impressive. They had quit their jobs and having saved enough (despite the expense of charter flights to Fair Isle; the Shetland Oil Companies must pay pretty well!) they were now 'doing the east': a fabulous six-month trip starting in Nepal, and ending up in Japan and taking in Malaysia, Thailand and, as it turned out, our mountain on the way! Twitching is sometimes a maligned activity, and with some justification (which I will consider in a minute) but if it leads young birders to organise themselves to the extent of being able to experience a once-in-a-lifetime trip like that – it can't be all bad. I envied them.

OK, so I said twitching is often maligned – by who and why? Well, by other birders, by farmers, and by the people who live on Shetland or Scilly. And why? Well, twitchers are accused of several faults, most of them based, I suppose, on over-enthusiasm. Full-time twitching is an *extreme* activity, and twitchers are *extremists*. Remember that guy's statement: 'If there is a new bird about – nothing will stop me seeing it – NOTHING!!' There's something almost para-military about that kind of mission. The competitive element which I claim (and I'm sure rightly) is an essential part of all birding is, in a twitcher, hyper-developed. Even the language of twitching has aggressive connotations. Oh yes, this is another thing – twitchers do have their own language. Many of these terms have passed into fairly general birding usage. They are extremely expressive, and since I shall inevitably be using them throughout this book, let's introduce and define them right now. (To anyone unfamiliar with this language let me here and now assure you that what follows is entirely authentic and not of my own invention.)

Glossary of twitching terms

A tick. The ultimate aim of twitching. Quite literally the tick you put alongside the name of a species when you see it. Some people use the species index at the back of their field-guide. Or you can buy one of the many available species lists published by the British Trust for Ornithology. Obviously ticks are related to the different lists you may keep – hence a British tick, a county tick, or a world tick (if you travel). The two most fundamental lists kept by most bird-watchers are British and world; and probably the list dearest to any birder's heart is his own British list. There have been (at the time of writing) about 470 species recorded in Britain. Not many years ago, if you had seen over 300 of these, you were doing pretty well. With the spread of twitching I'd say 350 was really needed to get people passably envious. One famous twitcher has recently achieved the magic 400.

There are certain rules generally held about what you are allowed to tick. Most contentious is probably the business

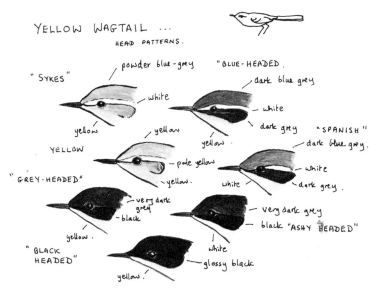

YELLOW WAGTAIL ...
HEAD PATTERNS.

"SYKES"
powder blue-grey
white
yellow

"BLUE-HEADED".
dark blue grey
white
dark grey
yellow

YELLOW
yellow
pale yellow
yellow.

"SPANISH"
dark blue grey.
white
dark grey.

"GREY-HEADED"
very dark grey
black
yellow.

white
very dark grey
black "ASHY HEADED"

"BLACK HEADED"
white
glossy black
yellow.

These are seven entirely different looking birds –
they are all Yellow Wagtails; and only one tick!
Hardly fair is it? If you'd like an almost
acceptable compromise ... if you see one of those
without an eyestripe ... perhaps that could
count as a second tick? Or half a tick?
Anyway, they're all worth seeing 'cos they
are very handsome.

P.S.   Well, they are in real life, 'cos they're in colour then.
P.P.S.   These are only the ones we get in Britain –
there's another "n" varieties round the world!

of sub-species and 'races'. I won't go into the biological and genetic complexities (because I don't understand them) but there are certain species that exist in more than one plumage form. The best example is the Yellow Wagtail. There is the basic Yellow Wagtail and there are any amount of recognisable races, seven of which occur in Britain, but they are all Yellow Wagtail, and if you are being hard on yourself you only get one tick no matter how many you see. On the other hand, if you count all the races as different you can add six more ticks to your list. The same problem arises with Pied and White Wagtails, Pink-footed and Bean Goose, Carrion and Hooded Crow, and Rock and Water Pipit. To be honest I really don't know what the official ruling is. I suspect *one* species is *one* species. So, if you're really being ruthless, there's no point in bothering to look at a Black-headed Wagtail because you can't tick it! This is sad because there is no more beautiful a bird than the Black-headed Wagtail. So take my advice, and if you hear that there's one about do go and look at it. Personally, I'd tick it too.

You are not allowed to tick a dead bird. This is not as silly as it sounds as rare birds are often found dead. They've usually flown a long way and when they finally realise they've pitched down in Hampshire instead of West Indies the shock is often too much for them and they snuff it. I mentioned the Yellow-billed Cuckoo earlier. There have been about forty recorded in Britain so it's not *that* rare a bird theoretically but the fact is that 50 per cent of them have either been found dead or expiring. Which is why the one that lasted five days at Portland was so gratefully received and widely viewed. I admit I used to veer towards a naughty and unacceptable principle that if *I* found a dead rarity *myself*, then it was tickable. A dead rarity does tend to get handed around or even preserved in a fridge, and you can obviously no more tick a deep frozen rare bird than one that is stuffed in a museum. But when, for example, as a boy, I found the remains of a Sooty Shearwater on a Norfolk beach, which, as far as I knew, had not been seen by anyone else, I was tempted to tick it. I have since unticked it – but then again, I have since seen lots of live Sooty Shearwaters. A couple of years ago, I found a Great Reed Warbler on the island of Out Skerries in Shetland – a new bird for me! God knows it hardly *looked* dead – its eyes were still open, it was still warm, and its reflexes were still operative. For half an hour I gave it the kiss of life. But I have to accept that I have a dreadful pang of guilt every time I see that tentative

EX GREAT REED WARBLER
Out Skerries, May '77.

tick on my list. It's only in pencil, but it's a sin, that tick. I shall rub it out soon. As soon as I see a live Great Reed Warbler. No, you *can't* tick dead birds.

Neither can you tick 'escapes'. This is another difficult area. There are plenty of birds that do occur as genuine wild visitors to this country, but are also kept in captivity. This is particularly so with wild fowl, and pretty-coloured buntings. By and large it's generally assumed that zoos and cagebird collectors only keep pretty-looking birds. This isn't, of course, entirely true. Some very boring birds have clearly spent much of their lives in cages before escaping and tempting us to tick them as genuine wild birds. You just have to be honest, and look for the indisputable signs of captivity. Be suspicious of anything that can't fly, although remember of course that wild birds can be injured, and they do moult, and then sometimes they can't fly. On the other hand, it's very common for keepers of wild fowl to clip the wings of their ducks, geese or swans, and if a rare duck has half its wing tips neatly sawn off, chances are that it's an escape. Other tell-tale signs that are hard to ignore are birds with conspicuous coloured rings on their legs; birds of prey with jesses trailing from their feet or hoods on their heads, and bald buntings. Most cage birds lose feathers, particularly around the beak where they have been trying to peck their way out of confinement. Also distrust birds that eat from your hand, run up ladders or talk.

So, you can't tick anything that has obviously escaped from captivity – unless it has become wild and been officially accepted to the British list. There have been several species that were originally ornamental or cage birds that have now established themselves in the wild and are therefore tickable, for example the Canada Goose, Mandarin Duck or Egyptian Goose and a couple of gaudy Chinese Pheasants. Every now and then, another species is promoted, like the Ruddy Duck. Some years ago a few Ruddy Ducks, and Ruddy Drakes, escaped from the Wild Fowl Trust at Slimbridge in Gloucestershire and now there are lots of them flying and breeding around the country. So many a birder gained a tick overnight with the promotion of the Ruddy Duck to the official list.

There is a little group of birds lurking in what is known as Category D. Category D lists: 'species which may have been escapes, found as tide line corpses which may not have reached Britain alive, or feral species breeding in the wild but not yet considered to be fully established'. So that last lot are well worth keeping an eye on. Whilst it's not really acceptable to tick a Category D bird and count it on your list, today's Category D bird is tomorrow's Category A bird and *then* it becomes a proper tick! (I'm not sure what happened to categories B and C. I think it's like the old British Rail, which used to have only first and third classes.) What's more, of course, birds are escaping all the time and beginning to establish themselves in the wild. There are quite a few free-flying Ring-necked Parakeets knocking around; and there used to be a flock of 'wild' budgies on the island of Tresco in the Scillies. So anyone wishing to get a few more ticks

American Ruddy Duck — looking very smug after just being admitted to the British List..

would do well to put a few packets of seed out for the parakeets and press for their promotion to the official wild status. I suppose if you are really desperate for a new tick there might be a case for campaigning for the release of more cage birds. If you could get all the canaries in Britain to break out they'd be up to Category A in no time.

So that is a tick. The twitcher's reason for living. I'm sure most twitchers are totally honest about ticks, but if you really want to be beastly, when they claim they're nearing 400, cross-examine them: 'Are you *sure* you are not counting any sub-species, races, corpses or escapes?'

So, on with the glossary...

A lifer. Much the same as a tick. An alternative term,

meaning the first time in your life you have seen a certain species, so it follows it must be a tick.

A megatick. A very good tick. Obviously any tick is good to the person who sees it, but the species doesn't have to be rare in the total context. Even the commonest species is a tick to the individual birder at some point but that doesn't make it a megatick. There's no definition but a megatick might be, say, a species that has occurred less than ten times in Britain.

An "impression" of a male Collared Flycatcher.
Definitely a "megatick" — and I've seen one!
So there!

A cosmic mind-f★cker. A very good megatick! Most probably a species never recorded before in Britain, and most appropriate to something that is not only very rare but looks fabulous too. I have personally recorded a new species for Britain – Pallas's Reed Bunting – but it was very grotty and brown and boring, and in no way would I have called it a cosmic mind-f★cker! Something really good looking and handsome, say a male Siberian Ruby Throat, or really big, like a Black Vulture, would justify such naughty language!

A first. Quite specifically a 'first for Britain'. Not just the first time *you've* seen it, but the first time *anybody* has seen it in Britain. So if a twitcher sees a first he's in for a megatick, and possibly ... a cosmic mind-f★cker.

To have a bird. Twitchers do not 'see' birds, they 'have' them. More usually, they use the past tense as they don't even like mentioning a rare bird until it has been safely ticked or had. Hence the phrase might be: 'I've just had an icky'.

A Pallas's Reed Bunting. A first for Britain &
I suppose a "megatick", but in no way a
"cosmic mind fucker". It is even more
boring in colour.

Which, being translated, becomes: 'I've just seen an Icterine Warbler.' (Twitchers have a slightly irritating habit of abbreviating birds' names, probably because it saves time which could be better used twitching than talking.) Use of this acquisitive 'had' instead of 'saw' I think emphasises the almost aggressive possessiveness of the twitching experience.

It also has connotations that are slightly excretory.

'I've just had an icky.'

'And I hope you feel better for it!'

Or sexual: 'I have just had a shag.' (There's no answer to that!)

Or even medical. My favourite in this category came from one of the Shetland group we ran into in Thailand. They had just journeyed up from Singapore. They informed us: 'We had fin-foot in Malaysia.' They seemed to have recovered, not even a trace of a limp! A Fin-foot is in fact a large ugly and rare water-bird.

This is a male Siberian   Rubythroat – definitely
a "Cosmic mind f*cker" if it ever occurred in Britain,
which so far, it hasn't. There have been two grotty
females (or immatures) recorded, but neither of them had
nice dazzling ruby throats. Mind you, neither has this
one ; which diminishes the extent to which this
drawing is f*cking your mind right now no doubt.

A sibe. Abbreviation for a 'Siberian', which means a species which breeds in Siberia and which would normally migrate between there and say India or Southeast Asia; but, through vagaries of weather conditions, or bad navigation, such species do occasionally turn up in Britain, particularly on Fair Isle or Scilly. They are invariably rare and invariably ticks and therefore in much demand by twitchers. And be honest there *is* something rather glamorous about the idea of a little bird which *should* be in Siberia flitting around in a field in Britain.

Burn up, or flog. You can burn up or flog an area looking for a bird; or indeed you can burn up or flog the actual bird! Either way the process needn't be quite as violent as it sounds! Basically all it means is to look thoroughly for the bird you want to see. Not surprisingly birds are often difficult to see, and they may well even hide from the 200 twitchers who are trying to have them. If, for example, a rare bird is originally spotted in an oak tree in a large area of woodland it is not entirely unlikely that the bird won't actually stay in the same tree. It might move to another tree. In which case the twitcher or twitchers will burn up or flog the whole woodland until the bird is relocated and had.

Burn up is purely figurative, and I have never seen any twitcher actually set fire to woodland in order to expose a bird.

Flog can be pretty accurate, as it is common practice to gently (or even roughly) flog or beat bushes or trees in order to chivvy the bird into the open so it can be had. As I said the verb is often used transitively, so that if, let's say, an 'icky' was eventually flushed from the woods you might say: 'I've flogged the wood and burned up the icky.' OK? I know all this sounds almost cruel, but really it isn't . . . well not usually.

Dip out. To fail to see the bird you wanted to see. This is the experience a twitcher most dreads, and it is sheer heartbreak. If I may give a personal example – I am an expert on dipping out. In autumn a few years ago I was filming a TV series in Cornwall. Cornwall is (coincidently) within dangerous twitching distance of the Scilly Isles, and on my occasional days off I would hop on to a helicopter and make

day-trips. Three times I went at weekly intervals, each time
in the hope of seeing a particular rare bird. The first week
there had been a Sharp-tailed Sandpiper (a pretty rare bird)
in residence at a certain field along with three Pectoral Sandpipers (which are not so rare). I arrived at the field two hours
after the bird was seen for the last time after a two-week stay.
During the same period there was a mysterious elusive
warbler seen regularly in a nearby patch of reeds. I arrived
the next week only to hear that the bird had at last been
caught and identified – as a Paddy-field Warbler (very rare,

An "Icky" — what's the poor
bird done to deserve being called <u>that</u>!

four British records). It had been caught on the evening
before my visit and released, and was never seen again. Just
to make the experience a little more galling the bird had been
trapped with *my* net, which I no longer use, and had donated
to a resident Scilly birder. So the following week I tried
again. I passed a pleasant day on St Mary's island seeing a
few birds but nothing startling. I was on my way back to the
heliport when news came of a Pallas's Warbler (a not only
rare, but very pretty bird). I literally ran to the spot where
it had been seen, which turned out to be the same spot where
I'd sat and eaten my packed lunch and seen or had nothing!
As I tagged onto the back row of three ranks of twitchers

Pallas's Leaf Warbler – seen here
assuming an undignified & uncomfortable
posture for the sole purpose of
showing off its good points so I
can draw them in black & white –
What a waste of effort !

P.S – the dark bits should be olive &
the pale bits yellow . . . .

and raised my binoculars, I saw a flash of yellow rump disappear into the woods like a rat up a drainpipe – and that
was that. It never reappeared. That was dipping out. The
verb is used thus: 'I dipped out on a Sharp-tailed', 'I dipped
out on a Paddy-field', and 'I dipped out on a Pallas's'. Note
that the twitcher doesn't bother with the second part of the
bird's name either. In this case, 'sandpiper', 'warbler', and
again 'warbler' are all implied and understood.

Being gripped off. This is by no means as pleasurable as it sounds. You may equally use the phrase – being seen off. Either way, its a nasty experience. It means *you* have dipped out, but somebody else hasn't. In other words, a rare bird has been reported. Several twitchers go twitching for it – some of them see it – but *you* don't. The others have thereby gripped you off or seen you off ... and it hurts!

There is a dangerously uncharitable implication in the fact that the verb is also used transitively. You can grip somebody off or see them off. This is bringing the competitive element right out into the open. In other words, the twitcher admits that he may derive pleasure from getting one up over his fellow twitcher by seeing something which the other fellow hasn't. When it becomes a bit nasty (and it does) is when you (*a*) suppress information or openly dissemble. For example, when asked 'is there anything about?' You answer: 'No.' (When you know damn well there is!) Or even: 'Is it (the rare bird) still there?' 'No, it's gone.' (When you know it hasn't.) Or (*b*) Less actively, you simply neglect to spread the news of a rare bird. Or (*c*) You try and scare the bird away so no-one else can see it. Many a twitcher has been caught hurling stones at a rare wader. They'll usually claim they are trying to make it fly so they can see its wing-pattern or rump or hear it call (whatever noise it makes probably translates as 'Please stop throwing stones at me'). In fact what's going on is an attempt to terrorise the bird into flying back to Siberia before the rest of the twitchers arrive and tick it.

So being gripped off isn't nice and neither is gripping someone else off.

Duff gen. False information. A rare bird has been reported and a description of it given to support the identification. When you get there you discover that the bird isn't what they said it was at all. It's not a rare one, it's a common one that someone has misidentified. You have thereby been given duff gen. The term may also be applied geographically. For example, you may have been told a first has been sighted in Scilly and you twitch all the way down there, only to discover it was in fact seen on Fair Isle – again you have been given duff gen, *and* you may also suspect you have been well and truly gripped off!

String. This is a really good one, and complicated, so concentrate! Let's give an example: someone reports a rare bird and presents you with a description of it to support his identification. You suspect that the description is in fact duff gen. In other words he has made an erroneous identification. Perhaps you even question the person who found the bird, and suggest that he might have made a mistake. However, despite the doubts raised, the original observer sticks to his guns and claims that the bird really is what he says it is. You don't really believe him. Thereby you consider his record to be stringy. He is accused of stringing the bird, and if he does it again he is labelled as a stringer! It is not good to get a reputation as a stringer. Basically it means you are considered to be an unreliable observer. Alas, such reputations are often unfairly earned, quite simply because there is a tendency among some twitchers to disbelieve anything they dipped out on. They don't *want* to believe that they have been seen off. So many a good record is dubbed as stringy quite simply because the bird didn't stick around to be seen by more than one person.

On the other hand, stringy records *are* rife, whether borne of over-enthusiasm or incompetence. It is a subject we shall come back to at greater length later.

For now, just assimilate the terms ... Stringy record ... to string a bird, or to be a ... stringer. None of them good news. OK?

By the way, I am not sure of the semantic derivation of the word. It may be a diminutive of the word ropey (meaning a bit tatty and unreliable) or it may have developed from the idea of stringing someone along, i.e. spinning them a yarn.

Dude. A posh bird-watcher, who doesn't really know all that much about birds. It is a terribly unfair term, used to dismiss all sorts of nice people who just enjoy watching or spotting birds, and don't take it too seriously. It is certainly derogatory, and reeks of inverted snobbery. The serious twitcher or even the serious birder quite values the purity of discomfort – getting up early, sleeping out, sitting in the rain etc. They all prove your integrity. The dude is not into discomfort. He potters out after breakfast, stays in cosy hotels and waits for the sun. Which only goes to prove that he is not really a *proper* birder, let alone twitcher. This is of course a grotesque over-simplification. As indeed is...

Twitcher. Somebody who is obsessed with ticks, races around the country chasing rare birds, and uses all the terms I have defined over the last few pages.

The fact is of course that many birders are all things at all times, or some things at some times. There are few of us who do not enjoy a little dude comfort, and few of us who do not indulge in a little twitching. On the other hand, there definitely *are* undeniable dudes, and undiluted twitchers, and these extremes do not mix well. I said before that twitchers and twitching come in for a deal of criticism, and I will try and examine why and whether it is justified. So I will! Let's ask the question – does twitching harm any one or anything? In the first instance, does it harm the bird?

Does twitching harm the bird?

The answer to this has to be very rarely indeed. Usually a rare bird has travelled thousands of miles and is tired, hungry and lost. Two hundred pairs of binoculars looking at it certainly will not embarrass it; it will be too busy feeding, sleeping or sadly, in some cases, dying. Harassing the bird will annoy it. It probably will not take kindly to being burned up. If it's fit enough, mind you, it will just fly away, and every one will dip out. There is no doubt, however, that if a weary migrant bird is constantly chased, flushed from cover, made to fly and prevented from feeding by the efforts of birders trying to see it, then that bird is being harmed. In my experience this does not happen often. Even when it does, I suppose one could reasonably claim that harassment by birders is nothing compared to the dangers of wind, rain, lack of food and predators; not to mention hunters, kids with air rifles, etc. Mass twitching can be irritating to the bird but it very very rarely harms it.

Does twitching harm property, farmland or local people?

This is the most delicate area, and in some cases the answer has to be yes. There are certainly some parts of Britain where birders are becoming *persona non grata* – most notably on the Scilly Isles, Shetland and Fair Isle. There have been many accusations of damage to property and crops. There is no doubt at all that damage *has* occurred, usually quite simply in the breaking of various rules of the Country Code. Dry-stone walls have been climbed over, collapsed, and not replaced; fences have been broken; gates left open; and crops have been trampled. It is particularly sad when this kind of abuse occurs in areas which are not by and large festooned with 'private' notices, nor fenced in with barbed wire, and where the local people have a genuine interest in and fondness for wild life. Many of the crofters on Fair Isle and Shetland know as much about the birds as the birders. They are enthusiastically informative about what they themselves see, and they are invariably generous and co-operative about allowing access to their land. It is really unforgivable, therefore, that a minority of twitchers have managed to antagonise these people and abuse their generosity. I was particularly saddened to hear of the events of a recent autumn on Out Skerries, a tiny island where I have stayed several times and seen excellent birds. No crop on the island is more than a few yards square and there simply isn't any area that a bird could hide in for long, and yet birders have impatiently crashed through growing plants. Equally, with an indefensible show of meanness, some of the same people who could clearly afford to charter planes around the islands kipped down in the local village hall for a week or so, made free with the electricity generator, and left making no contribution to the cost of oil or maintenance. Similar displays of thoughtlessness and selfishness have led to the banning of camping and sleeping rough on Fair Isle during the autumn. However, I am bound to say that the incidents are rare; most twitchers appreciate the Shetlands and the Shetlanders, and the Shetlanders actively enjoy the presence of the birders.

Not so in the Scilly Isles. In this case, however, I am very much prepared to defend the birders. Scilly is a wonderful place for rare birds, and consequently a wonderful place for twitchers. During October it's probable that there may be something like three hundred birders staying on the various islands, most of them scattered about the many hotels, guest houses and holiday cottages, a few camping, and a very few sleeping rough. Large areas of the Scillies are highly organised farmland, mainly for bulb growing. It is delicate terrain, very easily abused. It's all too easy to trample on growing plants which are hardly visible; and there are miles of stone walls and fences, and hundreds of gates. Little wonder that with three hundred frantic birders in pursuit of the most tempting rarities recorded in Britain some damage has occurred. Considerable wonder that the damage hasn't been greater!

In fact, regular Scilly birders have made considerable efforts to circulate a code of conduct, and develop a high standard of behaviour, and in recent years there has been very little damage indeed. Typical of improved relationships was the event of a couple of Octobers ago when a Red-eyed

Vireo (a very rare American bird) arrived on St Mary's. The farmer expressed no resentment when two hundred or so birders packed into one tiny field in ranks that resembled a full-house at the Wimbledon centre court. Fortunately the field was only long grass, but by the evening it was totally *flat* long grass. The birders organised a whip-round, and presented the farmer with a sum as compensation for the disturbance of his privacy and the flattening of his field (it really *didn't* look very nice). I believe the idea caught on to such an extent that when another rare bird turned up the next autumn in a more vulnerable area of crops, an arrangement was struck by which the farmer charged a small viewing fee, for which each birder was allowed ten minutes official 'trespassing'. Apparently it cost some twitchers quite a pocketful before they eventually came to grips with the bird, which was presumed to be a Blyth's Reed Warbler (four British records). Rather sadly, it turned out to be stringy and was eventually identified as a Marsh Warbler (not at all rare).

No, by and large, I reckon that birders on Scilly behave pretty well considering the emotional pressure they are under. And yet their presence is still resented by many of the islanders. So why should this be? I think the answer is that the arrival of three hundred men and women in khaki anoraks, all armed with binoculars and telescopes feels like a military invasion. Frankly, it must be pretty intimidating. What's more, the general atmosphere of the Scillies is rather sedate – fields of daffodils, yachts, holiday cottages and a few excellent hotels – all expensive enough to guarantee that the clientele is pretty affluent. To the islands' eternal credit, there is not a bingo hall or amusement arcade in sight. The Scillies *are* lovely and they are, in a thoroughly delightful sense, quite posh. So this khaki invasion-force really does seem a bit disruptive. Another analogy which I think is not inappropriate is that of the little village that hears it is about to be 'blessed' with an outdoor rock festival. Personally I think outdoor

rock festivals are great, but I can appreciate that the inhabi-
tants of a sleepy rural community, who probably think Pink
Floyd is a species of sweet pea, find the idea a bit frightening.
Above all, it is *mysterious*. Just so in the Scillies. I mean, what
are all those invaders doing? *Who* are they? *What* are they?
Yes, we know they're bird-watching; but why do they
always seem in a hurry; and why do they go around in huge
packs yelling to each other about 'sibes' and 'firsts' and being
'gripped off'? And when you wake up in the morning, you
draw the bedroom curtains, and there's a hundred pairs of
binoculars and sixty telescopes trained on your washing line!

No, they are not doing any *harm* but ... Two Octobers
ago a Scilly farmer put up a notice on his garden wall which
I think is the most honest statement I have ever seen on the
subject. It read: 'NOTICE TO BIRD-WATCHERS –
KEEP OFF HEDGES AND GATES. YOUR PRESENCE
IN LARGE GANGS IS BECOMING VERY IRRITAT-
ING'. Now I can understand that. To be honest, *I* was one
of those bird-watchers; but after a week on Scilly in October
I left vowing I would never go back there again at that time
of year. I can honestly say that it is the only time in my life
that I came near to wanting to pack up birding entirely. I
lost my enjoyment and I lost my enthusiasm.. The day before
I left, I dipped out on four ticks within a couple of hours,
and I couldn't have cared less. I just wanted to get away.
So I suppose this leads to the question...

Do twitchers harm other birders?

And again despite my response that October in the Scillies,
the answer really has to be no. The majority of those three
hundred in Scilly were doing what they wanted to do, the
way they wanted to do it. They were not causing damage,
and they were not preventing me from seeing any of the birds
I wanted to see. Arguably, they were making it easier – all

I had to do was wander around looking for the 'centre court' groups and I would be led instantly to the next rare bird. *I* was the odd man out (no pun intended).

Quite simply, it all gave me claustrophobia; and this, to a point, may stem from the fact that, being a so-called TV personality, I spend much of my life signing autographs, being stared at and generally being followed. I identified with Woody Allen when he said: 'I used to have this weird feeling people were following me – then I realised they were!' I don't get as many as Woody Allen (I'm sorry to say) but maybe enough for me to want to steer clear of fields full of twitchers (not that any of them were looking at *me*). I do prefer birding alone or with only a few other companions. So that's *my* problem, not a criticism of twitching.

However, I know many other birders who also prefer to steer clear of twitching packs, and, since *they're* not on telly, there must be more to it than paranoid claustrophobia. I think it hinges on an almost mildly moral contention of what the excitement of birding *should* be about. I can best illustrate this by referring again to another Fair Isle incident.

In June 1979 I spent a wonderful week at the bird observatory on Fair Isle, and during that time we were fortunate enough to have two terrific birds – a Spectacled Warbler (a third for Britain) and even better a Cretzchmar's Bunting (a second for Britain). These birds seemed to me to represent due reward for hours tramping round the island. Not so much for *me*, as for the warden and his assistants who work so hard keeping log-books, writing up records, trapping, ringing, carrying on the day-to-day running of the observatory, and not least, putting up with the many days when there are no rare birds around. The morning after each discovery, the Shetland twitching group was on the phone:

'Anything around?'

'Yes, Spectacled Warbler.'

And a few days later: 'Yes, Cretzchmar's Bunting.'

In each case by about ten o'clock the charter plane was zooming down on to the island and half a dozen twitchers were galloping around the field in a frantic search for what I suppose I considered to be 'our' birds. I can only say I resented it. I resented the noise of the plane's unscheduled disturbance of the peace of the island; but, more than that, I resented the fact that somehow I felt *we'd* earned those birds and now they were about to become just a tick. Well, as it turned out they weren't because neither of them was ever seen again! I can't pretend that, in a way, I wasn't quite tickled by that. But I *wasn't* just perversely enjoying the fact that we'd seen them off. No, honestly, it wasn't that. It was that somehow that plane and those twitchers had been an intrusion, and, what's more, it seemed almost morally wrong. *We'd* found those birds; *we'd* tracked them down, studied them and identified them. All the twitchers were doing was flying in and ticking them. I resented *that*, but ... I honestly think my resentment is totally unreasonable and unjustified – but it *was* real.

So what's the conclusion on this one? Do twitchers harm other birders? I have to say yes and I have to say no! The invasion of lots of people into a limited area which is *your* special study *is* disturbing and upsetting. I have talked to several observatory and reserve wardens about this, and they all admit they almost dread finding a rare bird, because they know there will be a flood of twitchers. But most of them also agree that, in a sense, they have no right to feel such resentment, and that, in a literal sense, the twitching is doing them no *harm*. So draw your own conclusion!

There is, however, one other group that twitchers could harm, and that is themselves – so let us finally ask ...

Do twitchers harm twitchers?

Well, yes, I think sometimes they can. Literally even. Certainly, they risk a few dangers; climbing cliffs, wading across quicksands, driving too fast – but that's all part of the game. They harm themselves if they do damage to farm property and provoke even more 'private' notices. But that's still not what I really mean.

No, it's that usual 'danger' – over-enthusiasm. It can lead, quite simply, to bad bird-watching. Inaccurate bird-watching. I suppose it's not really harmful, but it is a bit of a disease. A quick story to illustrate, told to me by a friend of mine. We shall call him Dave (because that's his name).

There had been a report of a White-rumped Sandpiper (a rare American wader) from a Midlands reservoir. Dave went to see it. He arrived to find a party of twitchers leaving the locality and asked them. 'Is the White-rumped still here?'

'Yes – over on the mud. It's the only bird there. You can't miss it.'

So Dave tramped round to the hide, overlooking a fair expanse of mud. In the hide was another birder with his telescope trained on a single small grey wader, asleep some way away. Dave looked at it.

'Is that it?' he asked.

'Yep,' came the reply.

'Why isn't it a Dunlin?' asked Dave (not so much aggressively as because he couldn't see how a bird asleep more than a hundred yards away could be so positively identifiable).

' 'Cos it's a White-rumped.'

'OK, but why?'

' 'Cos it's smaller than a Dunlin, and with a straighter bill and longer wings and the back pattern is different.'

'Have you seen the white rump?'

'No but you can see everything else.'

'OK.'

The bird remained asleep. The confident birder packed up his telescope. A few other twitchers came and went. They viewed the bird, ticked it off – 'White-rumped Sandpiper' – and also left. Still the bird remained asleep.

Dave descended from the hide and walked a little way along the shore. At which the bird woke up . . . and flew away . . . revealing *no* white rump. It *was* a Dunlin.

Frankly, there's plenty of stories like that, and no doubt plenty more occurrences that haven't become stories, because no one has questioned whether the bird that everyone is ticking really *is* the bird they have come to see. I wouldn't say it happens often, but it certainly *does* happen? It happens when the desire to get that tick outweighs the desire to actually learn how to identify the species. It need *never* happen if you follow a simple rule. If you go twitching and you catch up with the bird, just ask yourself two questions: Would I have been able to identify this myself? And will I be able to identify another one if I ever see one again? In other words, *never* totally rely on what someone else tells you. Be grateful for information by all means, and for heaven's sake listen to advice from them as knows, but always check it out for yourself. It's all to do with taking descriptions – but more of that later.

The bird on the left is a White Rumped Sandpiper asleep, and the bird on the right is a Dunlin, also asleep. Or is it the other way round? No, actually the differences are perfectly obvious. Note the more "scollaped" back pattern of the White-Rumped and the longer wings and smaller size. If they wake up you'll also see the shorter bill of the ~~Dunlin~~ White-rumped and if they fly you will see its white rump. On the other hand the bird on the left could be a small Dunlin and the bird on the right could be a large White-Rumped. Or they could both be something else entirely.

Here endeth the long long twitching chapter.

I have spent a long long time trying to examine the philosophy, motivation and language of twitching. I think it's vital, because I truly do believe there is a bit of twitcher in us all (in us birders I mean). If you are not a birder, then it is important that I should try to convey to you the depths of emotion and passion that are involved in chasing birds. Make no mistake, birding can be a marriage-breaker. It's just as possible to be a 'bird widow' as a 'golf widow', and if you are faced with the choice between for example finishing this chapter and going to see a rare ... sorry, must dash ...

Damn, dipped out again!

Now where was I? So what do *you* want to be? or what are you already? Twitcher, dude, or just a birder? The truth is that most people are a combination of everything – it depends on the time of year, where you are and what mood you're in. Or indeed you *can* opt to be a quintessential stereotype, because they certainly *do* exist. How do we recognise them? Simple, just like you recognise birds – study the plumage and take a description. What do they look like? What do they wear? What kind of equipment do they use? How do they behave? All this brings us to ...

3
Equipment and clothing

A FIELD GUIDE TO BIRD-WATCHERS

There are certain pieces of equipment and types of clothing that are common to all bird persons. The details (size, brand-names, colour etc. etc.) can give away a lot about your attitude, ability, experience and so on. The main object of all clothes and equipment is to denote the seriousness of your involvement in birding. There are plenty of tell-tale signs by which you can tell if a person is basically a twitcher, a birder or a dude – or, to be less factious, experienced or a beginner...

Binoculars

The essential piece of equipment. If you haven't got a pair of binoculars, you can only be categorised as a non-bird-watcher.

What do you call them? Binoculars is OK, but it's playing safe. Diminutives always indicate a certain hipness, hence bins – which is also very down-to-earth and workmanlike. 'Glass' is also acceptably élite; though, personally, I always think it sounds a bit posh or nautical or something. I cannot refer to my glass out loud without blushing. Considering that I embarrass myself so easily it's amazing that on the other hand, I am shameless enough to occasionally speak of my 'nockies'! Which is so twee that it sounds like something out of Noddy! (Bill Noddy? No forget it!) Anyway, with a bit of luck you won't have to decide which word to use. Don't mention them at all. Just make sure you've *always* got them with you – but the right ones! Ah ha . . .

So what *kind* of bins/glass/nockies? The first thing to accept is that size impresses no one! And that goes for binoculars too. We've all seen those adverts for binoculars in the Saturday morning papers. They are designed to impress people who know nothing by two things, and size is one of them. '*Times 25 magnification! – Wow!*' Anything that magnifies over ten times is bound to be so heavy that you'd need a crane to lift them up (a crane crane, not a bird crane). If you hang those monsters round your neck you'll walk with a permanent stoop and never see anything but your own feet – and birds don't often land on your feet. And probably you'll fall over a lot. And note too that, perhaps strangely, the *bigger* these binoculars the *cheaper* they are. '*Times 25 – Only £12!*' That's less than 15p per magnification! They are cheap because they are badly made. If you think about it, it's easier and quicker (and therefore cheaper) to bung great big lenses together than fiddle around with tiny precision parts. Look through them (if you can lift them to your eyes) and you'll find that they have blue or orange edges round both the birds you can see (there's actually only one bird there). And don't go out in the rain with them, because they'll let in water, and don't go out in the sun because they'll let in the dust. Just don't go out with them at all. Oh, and, don't be fooled by the fact that they have an impressive sounding German name. There is a general fallacy abroad that any good binoculars have a 'Z' in the name or possibly a 'SCH', or even better both! The makers of cheap binoculars know this. Look at that ad: '*Ex army Zoffel and Schuntz,* ×

25 Binoculars. Only £12!' Well own up, not only were the
German army not at all well known as bird-watchers, but
they *lost*! Probably many of them crippled by their own
Zoffel and Schuntz's.

So tiny poncy little binoculars are often very expensive and
good, and the big butch ones are usually lousy. However,
it's not easy to categorise a birder by his bins – all you can
tell is whether he's rich. Probably the best binoculars (or certainly indisputably good ones) do indeed have a 'Z' in their
name – Leitz and Zeiss (West Germany). (Oh by the way,
there are half a dozen different Zeiss's around, so be careful
there too.) They are small and rather effeminate, and very
expensive. So many a full-blown, wealthy dude has a pair
of Zeiss or Leitz, whilst many an impoverished twitcher
hasn't!

More of a give-away is how you wear your binoculars,
and how you treat them.

If you don't want to be considered dude you should distress
your binoculars, in the way that antique dealers distress new
paintings to make them look old. So make sure there's a bit
of dust or better still sand or mud on them, but not on the
lenses. Lenses are cleaned a lot, but under stressful circumstances, and so the lenses should be scratched a bit – clean
but scratched. In other words, show the world you *use* your
binoculars, in all weathers. To add further proof, buy one
of those little leather caps that slide over the straps and cover
the eye-pieces in wet weather – no doubt they're technically
called rain caps. This is an immediate indication that you are
not a dude – because dudes don't go birding in the rain.
Furthermore, the rain-cap is excellent material for distress-
ing. You can stain them with tomato soup, coffee, or blood;
scratch them, warp them, chew them (that proves how involved and emotional you get) and stamp your name on
them. Finally a nice piece of one-up-manship is to festoon
your bins with rings – bird rings that is, not diamond rings

or ear-rings (I think that would be considered dude). The rings are supposed to have come from corpses of rare birds found along the tide line, but if necessary, you can nick them from bird observatory ringing rooms – but you really shouldn't.

Even more significant is *where* you wear your binoculars. It's likely to be round your neck, I know that (though I have seen binoculars slung over the shoulder) but how *long* is the strap? Binoculars *should* be on a *short strap*, nestling high on your chest – a minimum distance from your eyes. Make the strap *too* short, and you will not be able to get them up over your chin, and you'll probably knock your teeth out. The straps that come with the binoculars are always too long, and usually you can't shorten them enough without tying knots in them. Dudes never get round to this, perhaps because it spoils the smoothness of the leather. So dudes wear their binoculars swinging down by their waist or even lower, like a sporran. This is not practical because it's a long way up to the eyes. It can also be very painful.

Dudes invariably carry their *binocular case* slung round their shoulder. Even worse they sometimes carry their binoculars *in* the case. Definitely *soppy*. The case should have been lost long ago; if indeed you ever had one. Or alternatively, it might be used for carrying your packed lunch, tobacco for rollups, or one of those tide-line corpses. If you're really worried about your image – it's safest to throw the case away.

Telescopes

Even to *own* a telescope proves you are not a dude. So you really should get one. (By the way, I am sort of presuming you don't want to be seen to be a dude. This is actually very presumptuous of me; because it's very nice being a dude, and, by and large, they are happier than twitchers and often very pleasant people. Anyway back to telescopes.)

The hip word is scope. And you don't look at a bird through your telescope, you just 'scope' it.

Telescopes are dreadfully hard to look through, as the eyepieces rarely seem well suited to human eyes. There are many people who have eyes which simply don't work with telescopes. Though they may own one, they can't see anything through it, and never have been able to, but they are too embarrassed to own up.

Whether you can actually see through your telescope or not, there is still a certain snobbery attached to telescopes. There is a definite worthiness about discomfort. Hence you get quite a few marks for lugging around one of those extremely heavy brass telescopes like Nelson used to use. (Broadhurst Clarkson make them – or used to.) They pull out to such a length that you can look through them by lying down, applying one end to your eye and propping the other end on your feet. This is very uncomfortable, and proves you're really prepared to suffer for your art. Nowadays though most birders are willing to accept that owning a telescope at all is quite *cachet* enough, and they choose to use one of the many lightweight short models that are available. These are so short that only a midget can lie down and prop them on their feet (*I* can do it, but it really is painful). So the sensible thing is to carry a tripod. I've a feeling this is considered by some to be a bit soppy, but console yourself with the fact that tripods are awkward and often heavy and frequently fall to bits – so *you're* suffering too.

So that's it for what you look through. In the hope of getting a free supply, my personal equipment is: Binoculars – Zeiss 10 × 40. Telescope – Kowa, with × 20 wide-angle lens, on a Slik tripod. My only complaint is to Zeiss – the rubber eye caps become warped and misshapen, and the bins don't focus close enough. So onto clothes ...

Anorak

It needn't be *exactly* an anorak. Some kind of weather-proof top garment with lots of pockets is worn by all bird people. Some of them are definitely dude.

Bright-coloured anoraks – orange is a favourite – are a bit of a give-away; and, be honest, pretty silly things to wear if you are trying to camouflage yourself from birds. But being the right shade of khaki or shit-brown is not enough. Avoid *smoothness*. There's a certain kind of jacket that is undeniably dude. You'll see them advertised in *Country Life*, or any of those magazines you get in dentist's waiting rooms, or even bird magazines. They are dark green, and very smooth, with tartan linings, and lots of zip pockets. They are often advertised as being '*especially for the bird-watcher*'. Usually they are actually fishing jackets or point-to-point coats, or something. Those pockets that claim to be for telescopes are actually for collapsed fishing rods or riding crops. These jackets are probably warm, comfortable and practical, but if you wear one, you are a dude. That's up to you.

There is a safe rule when it comes to birding gear. Seriousness is in inverse proportion to cleanliness. So again you should distress your anorak (if you buy an ex-army one you'll have a head start). Otherwise if you get a new one, smuggle it home and pour oil on it; leave it out under a starling roost so that it gets spattered with bird shit (if you live in London amble round Trafalgar Square in it), and tear it a-bit.

Actually, one of the most versatile of garments is the heavy waterproof type of outdoor jacket (again often used by fishermen). The price, pedigree, comfort and efficiency is dude, but this is counteracted by the fact that it is instantly greasy, smelly and unpleasant.

Other clothes

Generally wear twice as much as is appropriate to the weather conditions. The heavy birder (and twitcher) probably has on *several* old sweaters, but you can't be sure because he never takes his anorak off – even on the hottest day. So actually it doesn't really matter what you wear under the anorak, because you can only see the bit exposed at the neck. An Irish knit dicky could well cover that exposed bit. Definitely no ties or cravats (though I suppose a tie with a polo-necked sweater would be considered characterful).

Head gear

This is another area in which it's hard to tell the dude from the twitcher, as ratting caps and deer-stalkers, flying helmets and even toppers are considered acceptably eccentric. Don't *ever* use the hood on your anorak; and, if you do, for heaven's sake don't pull the string tight so that you peep out like a little baby in a siren suit. That is definitely *soppy*; and significantly unserious, because you can't see or hear any passing birds.

Otherwise, I really have seen twitchers wearing the lot – from ten-gallon hats to bowlers. Some are more popular than others – woolly rasta hats are high on the list, as are little floppy khaki ones; and there's instant one-up-manship in wearing an authentic Fair Isle knitted hat. But whatever you wear, there are two rules –

The first is *cover the head gear with badges* and stick a few feathers in it, preferably from a rarity. If you've been present when a rare bird is trapped it usually sheds a few feathers, or sometimes they leave a few behind when they are being burned up. Or you can use hen feathers, and lie.

The second rule is *never take it off* even if it's a thick woolly hat and the temperature is over 80°.

Trousers

Not essential. Lack of them would indicate that you've got your priorities right, as they are in no way integral to watching birds. If you do choose to wear trousers you are safest with jeans; again distressed, patched and stiff from lack of washing.

Waterproof trousers are not only soppy but soggy and very unpleasant – unless you're into rubber. The matching bright orange waterproof kit – anorak with stringed hood and big baggy trousers is *right out*.

Footwear

Many birders never take off their wellies, and this is pretty safe image-wise. It implies you have no interest in sartorial matters or comfort, and that you expect to get wet. You should turn down the tops of your wellies. It somehow denotes a degree of athleticism and hardiness (letting the air get to your calves) and it makes sure you get even wetter.

Nasty unpolished toe-crushing boots are equally acceptable, but don't let anyone see you wearing neat woolly knee-socks.

Old track-shoes also denote the correct worthy degree of suffering. They are, of course, totally inappropriate and impractical, cold, not at all waterproof, and very painful, as you will often have to kick bramble bushes and dry-stone walls. So track-shoes are definitely OK.

If, as I suggested, we accept that the object of your appearance is to denote seriousness, then it is best indicated by torn and tattered garments, because they imply that you have had to run an assault course – barbed wire, water, gun shots, walls, brambles etc. – to see your birds.

There are a few other items you may choose to carry. A

stick for walking with or sitting on is dude. A stick for thrashing bushes (to scare the birds out or to vent frustration on dipping out) is OK. On the other hand you can thrash bushes just as well with your telescope, or kick them with your wellies or track shoes. Don't carry an umbrella unless you use it *exclusively* for thrashing bushes, preferably in the rain.

There are many optional extras birders often have about their persons. Knives, lenses, clothes, fags, Polo mints, old apples, hundreds of crumpled paper hankies – they are all just fine, as long as they are all stuffed into pockets so that your anorak bulges and sags. Never never carry bits and pieces in one of those soppy little rucksacks. If you *must* carry a rucksack it should be ungainly and with a metal frame and *huge*, even if there's only a packet of fags in it. This implies that you are really *moving around*, probably sleeping rough, and probably off birding to India the next day.

One final piece of bird gear etiquette. Remember those posh country jackets advertised specially for the birdwatcher? Well they often feature '*a pocket for your field guide*'! Oh what a giveaway! *No birder carries a field guide* (I shall discuss field guides and bird books later, by the way). No – you don't carry a field guide, because you don't *need* one, because you *know* what you are looking at, and, anyway, even if you don't – it's *cheating*. You are supposed to take notes and look it up later. Fifty totally puzzled twitchers arguing about the identification of a bird none of them have ever seen before will still pour scorn on he who produces a book and solves the problem on the spot. It just isn't any fun, and *you mustn't do it*. So, whatever you keep in that pocket, it *mustn't* be a field guide, especially not poking out so everyone can see it.

What you *should* keep in your pocket is, of course, *a notebook*. It is equally a give away if you *don't* carry a notebook. There are lots of types, from little ring-bound pads to the backs of cigarette packets. There is still room, mind you, for some enterprising firm to produce the *ideal* field notebook

– which opens vertically, has a page marker, blank opposite pages for drawing on, and an attached pencil that doesn't fall out and get lost. Actually the nearest to that currently available is a policeman's notebook (yet I don't know any policeman birders). But their notebooks do make excellent bird field notebooks. What's more, they can be a pretty good defence if you are on private land, as the irate farmer might think that you are a plain clothes detective and not throw you off.

So – equipment/clothes – take your pick and choose your own. When all's said and done, there are only a few *essentials* for birding and they are contained in the little list I always check before I set out: binoculars, telescope, notebook and a pencil, that's all you *really* need . . . oh and birds of course. And at last that is what we're coming to next. But before we get to that, let's make sure you've understood everything so far . . .

'TWITCHER', 'DUDE' or 'BIRDER'?
DO YOU RECOGNISE THE SPECIES? – DO YOU
RECOGNISE YOURSELF?

[Descriptions taken from 'A Field Guide to the Bird-watchers'. Pub. Oddsocks Press © 1980]

..?.. A pair shown here ... male and female, both adults. The female is the one shown in rear view. Immatures are very rare and are perhaps indistinguishable until they acquire adult plumage.

Plumage: One of the few species in which the female is more conspicuous. ♂ has bushy eyestripes. Eyerings (if present) – gold rimmed or tortoiseshell. Upperparts: ♂ – smooth green with lots of zips and possibly sheepskin trimmings. ♀ – bright orange, blue or yellow. Plumage makes distinctive rustling noise when moving.

Underparts: ♂ – nice tweed. ♀ – tartan, pleated.

Legs: variable, but always warm. Feet: real calfskin. Invariably nice and shiny.

Voice: ♂ – a considerable range of 'fruity' noises. ♀ – often utters a soft appreciative 'aaaw'.

Distribution: Usually seen in small flocks. Slow-moving, and often travels in a disciplined line behind a 'leader'. Feeds on five-course meals and agreeable wines.

..?.. Immature male shown here. Females are virtually unknown, which may well mean this is an endangered species. There may be a case for conservation – on the other hand there may not.

Plumage: Crown, ear-coverts, lores and chin – all woolly and hairy. Eyerings – red, through lack of sleep. Upperparts: dirty brown or dull khaki, or both. Underparts: tatty denim blue. Feet – white with three blue stripes but usually obscured by mud. Whole plumage heavily abraded.

Voice: Often obscene. Migratory call, an anxious: 'Anything about?' In full cry: various raucous noises with high content of profanity: 'Where the f*ck is it?', 'Jes*s, look at that eyestripe', 'Sh*t, I've dipped out', etc etc.

Distribution: Highly eruptive species. Usually found in large flocks. Covers vast distances at high speed in search of ticks. These flocks can cause damage to crops and in plague years can be considered a pest. Actually eats very rarely; many of them are scavengers.

P.S. Much nicer than they look!

N.B. Any similarity between the individuals portrayed here and real people is based on years of observation.
By the way, I know which one *I* look like! Oh what a give-away....

Bill Oddie.

F.G. ♂

..?.. A full grown male shown here. Adult females are not often seen, but the number of immatures suggest the species is doing well.

Plumage: Overall plumage is very variable, often showing characteristics of other species. Hybrids are frequent.

Head pattern: also variable but usually shows black eyerings from constant use of rubber eye-cups.

Upperparts: usually crumpled khaki green. Underparts – brown, green or denim blue. Feet: welly-boot greyish, often with whitish leg ring.
Altogether a bit boring to look at!

Voice: Often silent; but capable of a garrulous 'chattering'.

Distribution: Widespread. Solitary or in pairs, occasionally small groups. Some individuals and local populations are very sedentary. Others are predicably migratory, usually to the far North in spring and the South West in autumn. A proportion move East at all times of the year. In winter there may be some hard-weather movement to Southern Ireland.

Food: a particular fondness for Marmite sandwiches and 'ploughman's' ...

And here is a little questionnaire to help you sort out who's who...
1. Which of these birds would be a tick for you?
(a) Nuthatch (b) Red-throated Pipit (c) Pallas's Reed Bunting
2. Which of these birds would you most like to see?
(a) Nuthatch (b) Red-throated Pipit (c) Pallas's Reed Bunting
3. You have just had a Ruby-throat; have you...
(a) Cut yourself shaving?
(b) Been sick?
(c) Seen a cosmic mind-f*cker?
4. You have just been shown a little brown bird and been told that it is a Blyth's Reed Warbler – but it flies away before you get a decent look at it. What do you do?
(a) Tick it (b) Don't know (c) Don't care.

5. It is the last day of your holiday on Scilly in autumn; which of the following activities do you choose?
(a) Go to look for a possible Raddes' Warbler on St Agnes.
(b) Go to any island but St Agnes.
(c) Go on the 'Sea-bird Special' boat trip to look for Puffins.
6. Place the following in order of importance:
(a) Food (b) World peace (c) A Lanceolated Warbler

ANSWERS: If you don't know the answers – re-read the previous chapter.

4
Identification

What bird is that?

The fundamental ability every bird-watcher requires is to be able to identify the bird he or she is watching – agreed? No bird-watcher is happy if he doesn't know what he is looking at. I have already suggested that twitchers may spend much of their birding life looking at birds that other people have already identified for them; but no twitcher would deny that the greatest thrill of all is actually finding and identifying a rare bird for yourself. Anyway, *all* bird-watchers have to face the problem of sorting out an unfamiliar species. It doesn't really matter if the bird is literally rare or not – if you can't identify it, then it is in a sense rare, at least to you. If you've never seen a chaffinch before, then you won't necessarily recognise it when you do see one. So you have to watch it, study it and sort out its identity, just as you'd have to do for a genuine rarity. The process is the same – a conclusion has to be reached, and somebody has to be convinced that you have reached the right conclusion, even if it's only yourself. The opportunities for deception are endless. If you make a mistake you may be deceiving yourself. If you pass on the news of your sighting you may be deceiving lots of other people too. There is an initial question to be considered here:

is it best to bird-watch alone, or with other birders? Frankly, the lone birder is always a bit under suspicion. If you, alone, claim to see a rare bird, then other people are apt to disbelieve you – at least until they've seen it as well. You might assume then that it *must* be more relaxing and perhaps more efficient to watch birds in groups, but there are disadvantages. Groups tend to talk to one another and make more noise and, despite more pairs of eyes, I am not at all sure that they see more birds. Not only that, but if the group is largely concerned with ticking off rare birds, the determination to see something good can be so great that mass hallucination is quite common. In other words, a group's record can be just as stringy (remember that word?) as an individual's.

I think the only way we can really examine the processes and problems is by tracing the course of a mythical sighting. So let's assume you are birding on your own and you see a bird you do not recognise. We'll also assume that you are a reasonably knowledgeable birder. You don't recognise the bird, so the chances are it's quite a rare one. You are going to have to identify it and, if it really *is* rare, convince not only yourself but other people as well. So here you are . . . you and an unidentified bird. The pressure is on . . . So what do you do?

You can run away and forget you ever saw it. This certainly happens. It's really quite justifiable if, say, the bird flies over and gives you only a very brief view, and to be honest there's no way you can really be sure what it was. Even if you thought, 'Well, it *looked* rare', it might still be best to forget it. On the other hand, chances are you blurt it out to someone, and they'll suggest a possible identification, and, if it would have been a tick, there will be an awful lot of pressure on you to try to claim that you saw more of it than you actually did. If you are lucky, blurting out, 'I saw something I didn't recognise' might inspire other birders to find it and confirm its identity. If it turns out to be rare, you'll be glad. If it turns out to be common, you'll feel silly. It's your risk. So you *can* run away and forget you ever saw it.

But no, for this mythical example, let's assume you are getting a reasonable view of the bird and you are still not sure what it is. Clearly, what you do is – get out that field notebook and take notes and do little drawings. You do this *on the spot*, whilst watching the bird, or at least very soon afterwards. What you *don't* do is leave it till much later, and try to remember what you saw – because you won't be able to and you'll start inventing it, especially if you've begun to develop some theory about its identity. It's amazing how many descriptions are written after the birder has decided what he *hopes* he saw rather than what he *actually* saw. And it's suspicious how many descriptions seem as if they might have been copied or paraphrased from the text in a field guide. So – we are attempting to take notes on the spot. Genuine field notes. On the other hand, don't start writing immediately. It's true you should note the time, place, weather conditions, etc, but not before you have had a decent look at the bird first. Otherwise, you'll get a field note that reads:

> January 12th, Cley-next-the-sea. Just south of coast guard's tower, along shingle ridge. Wind – north-east, gale force three. Three-quarters cloud cover, after early rain. 12.15 hrs. First seen hiding in Marram grass. Basically an unusual . . .

You look up and the bird has flown away. So try to strike a happy balance between looking at the bird and accurately writing down what you see. It's amazing how difficult it can be to make accurate field notes. For a kick off, it's often surprisingly difficult to even write. 'January 12th north east wind' – probably freezing cold. Either your fingers are too numb to hold your pencil, or you are wearing big woolly mittens that reduce your hands to paws. And if you suspect a rarity you get over excited and your handwriting goes to pot! That's one of *my* problems. I have pages of field notes that are totally unreadable – it isn't my own shorthand or hieroglyphics – it's just scribble! I've probably lost lots of potential ticks because I couldn't decipher my own notes.

Doing quick field sketches of the bird can be very useful indeed but under pressure can be depressingly inaccurate, especially if you are looking at the bird, and not at the drawing. It becomes 'pin the tail on the warbler'. When you look down, it doesn't even look like a bird! I used to draw blank silhouette outlines of birds in my book, ready to be filled in with the relevant details. The flaw is that obviously you can't have a book full of silhouettes of every single bird family. It was OK as far as it went. I'd end up with a carefully-labelled silhouette of a bunting, with all the colour and markings well recorded, which was fine, as long as I remembered the note: 'P.S. This was actually a duck'. The basic shape of whatever you are seeing is one of the first things you note down. With any luck, it shouldn't be too problematical. At least you should be able to figure out whether you are watching a warbler or an eagle, or at least whether it was a big bird or a little bird. Actually, knowing to what family the bird belongs *can* present problems, and only experience can overcome it. As I shall later reveal, all sorts of abuses and misidentification relate to lack of accuracy about what *kind* of bird is in question. But for the moment, let's concern ourselves with making a description of what colour or colours the bird is, and which different bits of the bird are of different colours.

Which brings us to an understanding of the bird's anatomy. As with the human anatomy, you can be colloquial, or scientific, or very vague. So, with a man, you might refer to his head, his cranium, or the 'top bit', and it's just the same with birds. Here are two sets of field notes:

Crown – dark irridescent greenish black. Neck and mantle: dark, irridescent, with flecks of yellow, white and pale buff. Lesser coverts: dark green with pale buffish white tips. Median coverts with dark centres and pale tips, and greater coverts similar. All remiges pale on outer webs, purple tinges on primaries and secondaries and yellower on tertials. Retrices: dark greenish black. Lores darker. Ear coverts show paler green sheen No moustachial, malar stripe or supercilium. Pale whitish pink orbital. Underparts – throat, breast, belly and under-tail coverts all purplish black with a mauve tinge in front of scapulars. Bill – yellow. Legs and feet – dark pink.

Or alternatively:

A shiny black bird with a yellow beak. Looked like a starling.

Which is because it *was* a starling; and so was the first description.

You can, of course, strike a colloquial medium and write about upper parts, under parts, shoulders, wings and tail, etc, and this is what *I* did for years. To be honest though, even this is usually a bit too vague and I'm afraid there's no substitute for studying the anatomy and figuring out which group of feathers goes where, and what they are all called. Birds can be divided up, like those cuts of beef you see on the diagrams of bulls in butcher's shops. Most field guides include carefully-labelled anatomical diagrams, and it really is worth studying and memorising them, so that when you see a bird you can describe what each bit is like. It actually makes it easier to write the description (though you may need to work out a few abbreviations like – lesser coverts becomes 'L. covs' – and so on). You work your way along the bird, and it's a bit like painting by numbers. Which brings us to a very tricky area – *describing colours*.

You may have noticed the long description of the starling included such wondrously vague terms as 'buffish yellow' or

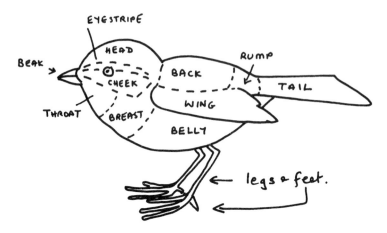

NB: If you do try eating the bird, make sure you spit out the beak. And, by the way, drumsticks on little birds don't have much meat on them.

PS: I am asked by the RSPB to remind you that by and large eating wild birds is WRONG.

'greenish black' or 'blackish green'. All bird descriptions in notebooks and in field guides are full of this sort of thing. There's never been a standardisation of colour description. I have heard it suggested that a colour chart should be published with widely accepted names like they have in paint catalogues. It's not a bad idea, but then presumably you'd have to carry it with you, and knowing how long it usually takes to decide what colour to paint the bathroom, how many birds would sit there long enough for you to match up the colour of their lesser coverts to the colour chart? No doubt paint-like names would also have to be acceptable. So we'd get such descriptions as: 'Lesser coverts – calypso yellow. Eye stripe – morning glory. Wing bars – Tahitian poppy' etc. etc. I suspect we're just going to have to carry on with buffish grey-white, blackish brown and so on. When you are really stuck, olive and buff seem to cover an awful lot of birds' upper parts, whilst whitish covers most of the under parts, but it's not awfully specific!

Taking good field notes is, without doubt, a fundamental skill and, frankly, there are no substitutes for thoroughness and experience. Experience is most useful when it means you realise the bird isn't rare at all, therefore you needn't take *any* notes. Experience is also knowing what bits are most important when you suspect the bird is rare. Either way, it's not my intention to cover in this book what has been thoroughly treated in many other books (see recommended list at the end and chapter on field guides). What I want to do is carry on with the experience of finding a rare bird.

Let's make another assumption in our mythical sighting. You have seen a bird and taken a full set of field notes. You look it up in a field guide and you are more or less convinced it really is a rare one. So what next? Whom else do you have to convince? If the bird is only new to *you*, you only have to convince *yourself*. But let's assume it's a real pukka rare bird.

Nearly every county in Britain has a bird club (we'll assume you are a member of *your* county bird club) and the bird club publishes an annual report of rare birds seen in the county. So there's probably a committee of local experts who will have to be convinced that you have really seen what you *say* you've seen. Or maybe you are going to go up the scale to national rarity status. There is a list of official rare birds published by the magazine *British Birds* and generally accepted by the birding fraternity in this country. The list includes roughly 230 species that are considered sufficiently rare for all occurrences to be documented and published annually in the *British Birds'* 'Rare Birds' issue. It is undoubtedly something of an ambition and an achievement to find and successfully report a bird that is on the *British Birds'* rare birds list. It is known as a 'rarities committee bird'. This is because if you *do* see what you claim is a *British Birds'* rarities committee bird, you have to submit your record to be con-

This is a page from my field note-book from some years ago. It records details of sightings of a Little Bunting and a Green-winged Teal. The Bunting was drawn on the spot whilst observing the bird. I filled in details of the Teal into a pre-drawn silhouette. The squiggle on the left is a doodle, and the reference, lower right, is to remind me to buy a new record I particularly wanted. I submitted neither bird as I have only just worked out what it was I think I saw.

sidered by – yes ... *The Rarities Committee*. This committee consists of ten highly experienced birders, who have, hopefully, an equal knowledge not only of rare birds but also of other birders. So what you have to do is send in the description of your rare bird and the ten 'rare men' have to judge whether you really did see it. They have to decide whether you are right, or whether you have made a mistake, or whether you are lying. They have an uneviable task, for as well as assessing the descriptions they have to deal with incompetence and deceit! Actually, it doesn't really matter if you are submitting your record to the county committee or to the ten rare men – the process and the pitfalls are the same. And the reward is similar – the satisfaction of seeing your expertise (and luck) acknowledged and the kudos of seeing your name in print in either the country report or *British Birds'* 'Rare Birds' edition.

I mentioned incompetence and deceit – well, yes, we have to admit both do exist. If all birders were equally knowledgeable and equally honest (with themselves and with others) there wouldn't be a problem. However there *is* a problem, and the problem most frequently occurs when you are not quite certain about your identification of the mythical bird, to which we now return.

If you are totally confident and if indeed you have identified the bird correctly, everything should be OK. As long as you write up an accurate description of what you saw, then everyone will be convinced and the record accepted. But let's assume you are not *quite* certain. So what do you do then? You can try to show the bird to other birders and get second opinions. This is what you *should* do, but if you do, you run the risk of being proved wrong. In which case you feel silly, and you lose a tick. So maybe you don't show the bird to anyone else. You pretend you can't find anyone else. Or you might even chase the bird away. This isn't as reprehensible as it ought to be, as many twitchers would sympathise with your determination to see them off. On the other hand they may not then believe your record. This actually doesn't matter too much as long as the relevant committee believes your record, so that it is accepted and published.

If the bird is only new to you and not a rare species you only have your own conscience to worry about. There are few birders who have not had stringy ticks on their lists at some stage. As long as the species isn't all that rare nobody will question it. I will own up that as a teenager I had a Black-throated Diver ticked off from a Midland reservoir that I know perfectly well was a Cormorant (and I think I knew it then). There was also a Haw-finch that was actually a poorly seen Chaffinch; and most ludicrous of all, a small flock of Black Grouse which I claimed to have seen from the back of a rugby coach in a field somewhere near Manchester! God knows what they really were – possibly cows? But none of these ever had to pass the scrutiny of a committee, only my own conscience, and they passed that OK for a shamefully long time!

But now let's get down to the real nitty gritty. You have a bird that is rare enough to submit to the committee, but to be honest you are not 100 per cent confident about it. Nobody else has seen it. By the time you got round to mentioning it to other envious birders and they raced to the spot where you saw it, it had gone. So it's *your* problem and *your* decision.

The really honourable thing to do is submit the notes you have, admit you are not sure, and let the committee make a decision for you. In fact this *is* done, but not very often. Few records are submitted with the heading 'I'm not sure what this was'.

It is surely an understandable human tendency that if you submit a record, you want it to be accepted. You therefore try to make the description appear convincing and your tone confident – even if you're not.

What I am about to go on to write is a trifle scurrilous, it even verges on ornithological blasphemy. Before I commit such scandal, I will reveal my sources to this extent – I have never served on an official rarities committee. On the other hand, I have frequently been in a position where I have had to judge other people's records (most birders judge other people's records all the time). I have talked with many experts who have served on various committees, and no doubt wish to remain anonymous, though I haven't asked them (come to think of it, they probably don't want to remain anonymous at all). Finally I have submitted *many* records to county reports and to *British Birds* and I am positively proud to say that in thirty years of birding I have only had a couple of rejections. I swear I have never consciously tried to get a record through that I felt was stringy. I will swear it but I can't be *sure* – such is the temptation, that it surely clouds one's integrity. I have certainly been tempted, and every birder *has*, and if you give in to temptation, you can justly claim that 'the balance of reason was disturbed' ... Such are the stresses involved!

Having guaranteed that I'll never have another record accepted again I may as well call this section ...

Fooling the committee

To submit a record you send in a description. You *don't* send in those unintelligible field notes. Rather like a policeman 'revising' his evidence to present to court, you write it up nicely, add a little here, take a bit away there, type it out neatly, and make it more presentable. And like the policeman's evidence, a description can be reworked judiciously to fit whatever facts you want in order to secure a conviction!

To continue the insidious police analogy – a description of a bird can be like an identikit picture. Most identikit faces look like nobody and everybody. Just so, an all-purpose description of a bird can be made that will fit more or less *any* species. Let's illustrate this wicked process. OK, here are three little pictures and a description:

SKYLARK

RICHARD'S PIPIT

PECTORAL
SANDPIPER

And here are the same three species
feeding in long grass, a long way away . . . .

Place – Cornwall, near Penzance, about half a mile from the sea. Date: October 10th. Wind: South, force 2. Previously cyclonic and calm. Warm and overcast. Locality: damp field with long grass and small flooded pools, near small airport. Size: Medium – about 7″ long? Upper parts – brown. Crown – streaked with darker brown. Mantle: heavy dark streakings and paler braces down the sides of the back. Wings showed more pale edges to the feathers and a generally scalloped look. Whitish eyestripe. Underparts: white with dark brown streaks on the breast forming a line across the breast in contrast with the whiteness of the belly. Legs not well seen, but looked yellowish, pale flesh?

Now that's a very basic description. It's not very full, but it doesn't sound entirely incompetent. It equally well describes a Skylark (which is very common), or a Richards' Pipit (which is quite rare) or indeed a Pectoral Sandpiper (which is also rare) and it's not a bad account of a hamster ... or a clothes brush! The secret is what you *leave out*. And *what name* you put on the page above the description.

Let's play a really silly game. The bird was in fact a Skylark. But we are going to try to pass it off as a rarity – either a Richards' Pipit or a Pectoral Sandpiper.

The locality is well enough chosen. Cornwall is but a twitcher's hop from the Scillies, and almost as famous for rare birds. The actual terrain is splendidly versatile: marshy grass with little pools, perfect for pipits or marsh-loving waders; and there's the nice touch of it's being within flitting distance of an airport. West Country airports are again famous for rare birds, as tundra-breeding species often mistake the cropped grass for their home countries. So, the location – authentic. Also the weather conditions: anticyclonic, calm weather, with a rather ambiguous wind direction – neither heavily from the east (which would be fine for Richards' Pipit but lousy for American Pectoral Sandpiper) nor from the west (which would be consummate with the Pectoral Sandpiper, but pretty unlikely for the Richards' Pipit). Anticyclonic means there is usually no wind at all, or it's all over the place, and in such conditions in the Scillies, I have certainly seen rare birds arrive from all points of the compass. So the weather description is favourable; it actually implies the presence of rare birds.

So let's be even sillier, and write Pectoral Sandpiper at the top of our description. Basically, it's not a bad description of a Pectoral Sandpiper! Note that there is no mention of the *shape* of the bird. Since you're claiming Pectoral Sandpiper, any reasonably generous-minded committee will *assume* it was some kind of wader. They will *assume* it had a long beak, long legs, and was wading around in wader-like fashion. You simply didn't bother to mention the obvious. In the same way that you didn't mention that it *actually* had a short beak, and short legs, and was crawling around in the grass. As I said – it's what you leave out!

You can improve your case by amending the description with an appealing combination of confidence and humility. In fact, you should show the confidence to be humble. So – you are still trying to pass off the Skylark as a Pectoral Sandpiper – you add to the above description – 'bill not seen properly' and, better still, 'leg colour obscured by grass'. This is a clever ploy. It shows you know the leg colour is an important thing to note and clearly you *tried*. You did say 'looked yellowish' – which is right for Pectoral Sandpiper anyway. And what's more, you will evoke sympathy for attempting to check it out. The mention of the bill somehow implies that although you couldn't see it (the bird was asleep perhaps?) the bird was nevertheless clearly a wader. The mere fact that you are admitting that you didn't get a perfect view makes you sound nice and honest.

If you can, try to incorporate the word 'jizz'. Jizz is a vital word that can win or lose the acceptance of a record. It's very mention is impressive – because it is doubtful whether it officially exists. Jizz is exclusively ornithological, so if you use it it shows you know a bit. It's not in the Oxford Dictionary and you can't put it on the Scrabble board. However, it is an essential and much used word in bird descriptions, and it means 'the general look or shape of the bird'. It is particularly used to indicate that a bird looks similar to another, usually better-known, species. So, in fact, if you are trying to pass a Skylark off as a Pectoral Sandpiper, you'd do well to avoid mentioning its jizz! Unless you are prepared to lie through your teeth, you'd have to admit that the bird you are dealing with has the jizz of a Skylark. Which brings us nicely on to the alternative deceitful identification. Let's now assume you've headed the description Richards' Pipit. The fact that you say the bird had a jizz of a Skylark of course implies that it wasn't *actually* a Skylark (even though it was). As it happens, a Richards' Pipit (being a big fat pipit) could well be said to have the jizz of a Skylark – so that's good, *and* you've authentically got that word jizz in. The rest of the plumage description fits very well with a Richards' Pipit. There's an additional nice touch in saying you couldn't see the legs because the bird was in long grass, yet clearly you *could* see the rest of it, including the underbelly, from which we may deduce that the legs must have been as long as the long grass. Richards' Pipit has long legs (you might care to enclose a piece of long grass). To be honest, you'd be better off trying to string a Skylark as a Richards' Pipit rather than as a Pectoral Sandpiper. You can happily mention its stout bill and white outer tail as well; but for Christ's sake keep quiet about the bloody great crest!

Another thing to keep quiet about generally is the *call* of the bird; it can be a terrible give away. In this case, if the bird kept flying to a great height and singing melodiously, best not to mention it. In fact, Skylarks make very few noises that could reasonably be passed off as Richards' Pipit. On the other hand, if you have the nerve to return to the original felony, Skylarks *do* make a call which can be described as 'a short slightly bubbly prrp', which would also be a fine description of the call of a Pectoral Sandpiper! The truth is, a Pectoral Sandpiper doesn't sound a bit like a Skylark or vice versa, but the limitations of phonetics have led both to go into the books as making a noise that is often written down as prrp.

Now, I'm not seriously suggesting that any birder has ever unwittingly or wittingly mistaken a Pectoral Sandpiper for a Skylark, though as it happens I'm damn sure some supposed Richards' Pipits have actually been Skylarks. Neither can I claim to know whether any Skylarks have got past the rarities committee as anything else but Skylarks. They are very shrewd, the ten rare men. But I do maintain that the psychology of what I have just outlined can be and is operative on a subtler level in the presentation of dodgy records. Birders may do it without realising – so try to be honest with yourself before you try being honest with the committee. You might as well, because those fellows know how to spot a stringer at work. Remember I said they not only have knowledge of birds, but also of birders. It is generally acknowledged that another impressive postscript which you can tag on to a description is: 'Observer familiar with the species' (this is supposed to denote that you've seen one before, either in this country or abroad and so can be reliably expected to recognise it again) but it isn't infallible – the record may well come back with a reject slip marked: 'Committee familiar with the observer'!

Every year *British Birds* also publishes, in its 'Rare Birds' issue, a list of rejected records; though it is discreet enough not to reveal the names of the people who sent them in. These rejections carry a diplomatic and tactful postscript:

> In the vast majority of cases, the record was not accepted because we were not convinced on the evidence before us that the identification was fully established; in only a few cases were we satisfied that a mistake had been made.

Oh what fun it would be to see some of those 'very few cases'! It is a tribute to the benevolence of the rarities committee that the stringy files are kept ever so secret. I would reiterate that I'm really not claiming that birders often (if ever) wilfully or consciously attempt to perpetuate a total deceit and get a record accepted when they *know* it's fiction. I *am* suggesting (naughty suggestion, though it is) that lots of records are sent in which really *shouldn't* be. When the observer really is, deep in his heart, pretty sure, if he's *really* honest, that though he's claiming to have seen a rare bird, what he *has* really seen is a common bird that *reminded* him of the rare bird that he would have preferred to have seen. If you see what I mean!

Which brings us back to that Skylark that looks reasonably similar to a Richards' Pipit, and is just a tiny weeny bit reminiscent of a Pectoral Sandpiper (if you don't look too hard). So what could have happened so far? Well, you've written up your description, headed it Richards' Pipit and sent it in. Maybe you got a card back from *British Birds* saying: 'Richards' Pipit, Penzance. 10th October, accepted'. That's it then. The ten rare men say it *was* a Richard's Pipit – so it *must* have been. Be honest, you'd had a slight doubt that it might just have been a Skylark, but *they* know more than *you*, so that's it. You've seen a Richards' Pipit. Tick. And when you see your name on that record in the 'Rare Birds' issue – I bet you'll blush!

Or you may get a card saying: 'Do us a favour mate – Richards' Pipit? You must be joking! Who do you think you are kidding, you stringer?!' Actually, *British Birds* don't send cards like that. You'll get that tactful stuff about 'insufficient evidence'. It would do you more good if they *did* put: 'Own up, it was a bleedin' skylark, you twerp' but they are nicer than that. And they are nicer than *me*, because having told you how you might be able to con the committee, I shall now tell you how to wriggle out of it if you're found out! We shall call this chapter...

5
Covering the cock-up

First of all, how has the cock-up been discovered or revealed? Well, it can happen right on the spot, before you've even sent in your claim. Let's go back to our mythical sighting again. You've been watching that Skylark, which for a moment reminded you of a Pectoral Sandpiper, but by now you've decided it's probably *not* a Pectoral Sandpiper, but it is *almost certainly* a Richards' Pipit. Half an hour later, you meet another birder who asks: 'Anything about?' and before you can bite your tongue off, you've said it: 'Yes, Richards' Pipit'. You may qualify a teensy bit: 'Yes, *probable* Richards' Pipit', but that's just as dangerous. In fact, it may be worse in a way, because 'probable' implies that you are not quite sure and the other birder will be tempted to cross-examine you. So he asks: 'Oh yes, good . . . where was it?' To which you reply truthfully, having not been given the time to lie: 'Er . . . in the field with the pools, near the airport.' To which he responds: 'Oh damn, I was looking there only half an hour ago. I only saw flipping Skylarks.' He then adds words which should be sad, but are in fact dreadfully accusing . . . '*I must have overlooked it.*'

You're probably trembling by now. You don't want to

admit that you've made a cock-up and you don't want to lose that Pipit – what you do want is ...

The two-bird theory

He gave you the clue as to how to rescue yourself by mentioning Skylarks S – plural – clearly there was *more than one* bird in that field. So what you are going to imply is that one of them was indeed a Skylark and the other was a Richards' Pipit, and that *he* saw the Skylark and not the Pipit, and *you* – lucky old you – saw the Pipit and not the Skylark? No no NO! You've got it wrong again. What *you* saw was the Pipit *and* the Skylark. So this exchange follows (and remember, this is the two-bird theory at work):

He says (significantly), 'Where *exactly* was the Pipit? All I saw was a Skylark, feeding over by the tractor.'

You reply: 'Oh yes ... there *was* a Skylark there, too.'

'By the tractor?'

'Yes.'

'Oh, actually, for a moment I thought it was going to be a Pipit, but then it flew up into the air, sang for ten minutes and dropped down like a stone and started feeding its young.'

'*That* was a Skylark.'

'Yes.'

'I saw *that* (which is true) *and* I saw the other bird – the Richards' Pipit (which is not true). There were *two* birds.' (This is probably also true: the truth is that there were actually six birds in the field – Mummy and Daddy Skylark and their four babies.)

By now you should be able to convince the other chap easily that so thrilled was he watching the Skylarks feeding their chicks (an understandably diverting sight on such a late date as 10 October) that he overlooked the Richards' Pipit half hidden in the long grass only two cows away.

You have now successfully executed the two-bird theory

and covered up your cock-up. (Sounds like a Kenneth William's line from *Carry on Birding* . . . mmmm now there's an idea. Sorry – back to the subject.) You use the two-bird theory, of course, when you are determined to stick by your claim and brazen it out. If you are *really* bold, you could even try it with Pectoral Sandpiper.

'Anything about?'

'Pectoral Sandpiper – in the field over there.'

'I've just looked there – I only saw a skylark.'

'Don't be *daft* – the *other* bird.' (Actually this is really quite safe – he can race back to the field and he'll see only Skylark.' and he won't for one moment think that you could *ever* have mistaken a Skylark for a Pectoral Sandpiper.)

'Damn, it must have gone.'

The two-bird theory takes nerve and determination, but it's quite convincing, particularly because it often turns out to be true! It's amazing how many little brown birds can hide in a field of long grass. If you'd tramped through it and burnt it up probably a dozen Richards' Pipits would have flown out, not to mention those four Pectoral Sandpipers . . . Oh, and a Skylark.

Of course there is another way the cock-up may be revealed. You may have had *an attack of conscience* . . . in which case, the quickest, but most painful, thing to do is to rush out into the street yelling: 'All right I admit it, it was a Sky-lark.' If you haven't sent the record in yet, that kind of beha-viour is really unnecessary self-flagellation; and even if you *have* sent the record in, it's still possible to get yourself off the hook without publicly humiliating yourself. All you need do is discreetly send a little note to *British Birds* asking if you can withdraw your record. They won't say no; and they probably won't even ask why. Which again proves how understanding they are. It's possible that the rarities com-mittee of today are the stringers of yesterday, so they know what goes on. They understand the hell and torment you've already been through. They'll just forget all about it. Mind you, they may jot your name down as a person to be suspicious of if you ever try to get anything else past them. But more likely, they'll actually admire your honesty. It does take a lot of nerve to be *really* honest and own up like that. Which is why few people do it At least if you *do* own up before anyone susses you out, you can give yourself time to figure out an *honourable* explanation as to why you made an *understandable* error. Actually mistaking a Skylark for a Pectoral Sandpiper isn't understandable at all. But mistaking a Skylark for a Richards' Pipit isn't *such* a terrible thing to do. But it will seem even less terrible if you can find some *extenuating circumstances*, especially if they are ornithologically diverting. Don't just say, 'OK it was a Skylark; I mistook it for a Richards' Pipit because I was upset that Arsenal lost at home.' You won't get much sympathy, except for having been to watch Arsenal. What you need here is . . .

The aberrant theory

Aberrant is a classy word meaning something that doesn't look quite the way it should. If you want to be a little more homely, you can substitute 'funny'. So in this case, yes, you're admitting the bird was after all only a Skylark, *but* it was a *funny* Skylark, or, better still, an *aberrant* Skylark. It *won't* work if you're still going on about Pectoral Sandpipers – there's a limit to how aberrant anything can get – but it's not too bad to cover up for Richards' Pipit. In this case the Skylark was aberrant to the extent that it had no crest, was surprisingly slim (through lack of nourishment perhaps) and had unusually long legs. It's not *very* plausible, but the Aberrant Theory always goes down well, because the fact that you know the word at all is quite impressive. Also I think other birders realise you are struggling a bit when you start talking about aberrants, and it is surprising how gracious they can be in not pursuing the matter. 'OK he's owned up, we'll let him off lightly. An aberrant Skylark? Yes yes ... very interesting ... never mind, we all make mistakes...'

Again, like the two-bird theory, the aberrant or funny theory has credibility, because it is based on fact. Oddly-plumaged types of common birds are frequent enough – albinos, that are all or partially white; melanistic types (black

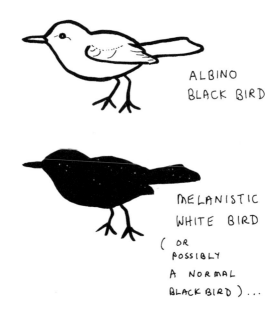

ALBINO
BLACK BIRD

MELANISTIC
WHITE BIRD
(OR
POSSIBLY
A NORMAL
BLACK BIRD) ...

ones); or leucistic (washed-out-looking). There's plenty of aberrants around ... plumage-wise. By and large though birds don't change shape much – although you *can* get extra big ones or unusually little ones. But still don't *ever* mistake a Skylark for a Pectoral Sandpiper. Actually, there's even a sort of one-upmanship to be gleaned from mistaking a genuine aberrant for something rarer. There are, for example, a few weird-looking robins around that look quite similar to Red-flanked Bluetails (which are very rare birds indeed). If you report what you think is a Bluetail, which actually turns out to be a funny robin, you can validly distract from your error by claiming that an aberrant robin is actually ornithologically more intriguing than a Red-flanked Bluetail. It's a good line – but give me a Bluetail any day! So, by now, I hope you are feeling a little better about making mistakes and hiding them. *All* birders do make mistakes, and it's a vital development in a birder's character to arrive at a point where he doesn't mind admitting it to himself or to others, and preferably while the bird is still visible. I can actually think of no more valuable trait than to be able to say: 'Oh that's a (rare bird), oh no, it isn't, it's just a (common bird).'

No one likes making mistakes, but it's comforting to realise that there are, as it happens, lots of mistakes that you can make that are really perfectly acceptable. It is openly acknowledged that some common species *do* look very like rarer ones, and they are pretty difficult to distinguish from one another. So you are allowed to mistake a common one for a rare one without too much stigma. These easily mistaken common species are a great source of fascination to the birder, and they are really very useful. The fact of the matter is you might go through the whole of your life without ever finding a rare bird at all, but fortunately you can send your heart a-fluttering every time you go out by *mistaking* one of these common ones – at least for a while. Which brings us to . . .

6
Brightening up a dull day

It's a dreadful thing for a birder to arrive at the week-end full of hope and expectation and then spend two days tramping over fields and marshes seeing bugger all! Alas, this is the way it often is. It is statistically provable that there are far more common birds than rare ones. Fortunately, there are many ways you can avoid being constantly reminded that this is so. The name of this game is . . .

Probables and possibles

You can play it by and with yourself or, rather riskily, with others. It's risky with others because not everybody may want to play or even know the game, let alone the rules. This is the game: it involves seeing or hearing a common bird very badly and briefly – this is important – and, at least for a while, *pretending* it is a rarer one. It is essential to know which birds are acceptably mistaken if seen badly enough. There was not much sympathy going for the lady who saw a Ringed Plover in flight and recorded it as a 'probable Alpine Swift' (that one apparently got as far as being submitted to the committee too!). Fortunately, as I said, there are *lots* of common species which are extremely versatile, and at a fleeting glimpse can resemble a rarer species, sometimes

several rarer species! Do remember, though, to see the bird
badly. The point of the game is to fool yourself and keep the
adrenalin going to carry you through a dull day. So, to go
back to our previous experience, if you saw that Skylark
really well, you couldn't honestly suspect it was a possible (let
alone probable) Richards' Pipit If, however, you saw it disappearing over the horizon about 200 yards away on a misty

One of these birds is an Alpine Swift
and the other is a Ringed Plover....
note the similarities ... and differences.
One of them runs around on mud and
sticks its beak in it, the other
doesn't, or if it does its in dead trouble.

day, you could *easily* be forgiven for pursuing it under the
heading of Possible Richards' Pipit. Got the idea? OK, so
now here's some practical help. Here is a selected list of common species that can, with very little effort, be mistaken for
rare ones. Skulking species are of course best of all, as it's easy
to see them badly. So here are some you may care to try for
yourself.

Dunnock. Try to see no more than the tail-end diving
into thick undergrowth. Don't pursue it at once, but dash
off and report a possible Lanceolated Warbler (about 25

"Possible" Dunnock.

British records), Pallas Grasshopper Warbler (five British) or Alpine Accentor (about 40 British Records).

Robin. A very versatile species indeed, as long as you avoid seeing the red breast. Some aberrant robins don't even *have* red breasts, so if you get one of those you're really in luck. Otherwise, convert your back view of a disappearing Robin into any one of many possible rare warblers; or small, and very rare, possible American Thrushes. If you can't ignore the fact that you did fleetingly glimpse the red on the breast, you can still try possible Red-breasted Flycatcher.

Wren. Try and see just a quick flash of dark reddish brown then hope it will peep out just for a second flashing its eye-stripe. You are then justified in mooting a possible Cetti's or better still, a Dusky Warbler.

"tchik"
"tchik"

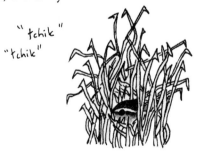

Eventual Wren.

Dunlin. A wonderfully versatile species that even when seen quite well can double as half a dozen possible American Waders. A small scrawny Dunlin (and Dunlins are frequently small and scrawny) can, even under close scrutiny, still be heralded as not only a possible but even a probable Broad-billed Sandpiper. It is best to see Dunlins some distance away on the mud (which they usually are) and try to ignore any noises they make which tend to be indisputably Dunlin-like. Fortunately there are nearly always other Dunlins around, so any noise you do hear can be blamed on some other bird. Dunlins really are terrific value, as they genuinely do come in lots of different sizes, which gives them a huge mistak-ability rating. Mind you, for versatility you can't really beat...

Domestic Pigeon. Pigeons have an uncanny talent for aerial mimickry. So, if you see one flying away in the distance, it can be justifiably mistaken for a wader, a hawk, a tern, or even a pigeon! The fact that domestic pigeons come in all colours and patterns makes them more or less unbeat-able subjects for the possibles and probables game. I have known of reports of Gyr Falcons, Greater Yellow Legs, Great Spotted Cuckoos, and White Winged Black Terns – all of which turned out to be pigeons!

In fact there are many many other common species that can be pursued in the possibles-probables game, and half the fun is learning by experience and becoming more and more subtle in your self-delusions. I assume you've now got the idea, so I won't spoil the fun by giving a comprehensive list. Discover them for yourself. I do reckon that if I have to choose a favourite, it should be possible, if you become an expert, to get through the whole day on one small scattered flock of domestic pigeons.

Talking of favourites, I do also have a favourite variation of the possible-probables game, and that is...

Mishearing bird calls

There is something almost infallible in this variation in that you needn't ever be found out or have to own up. If a bird just flies over and calls once, and you don't even *see* the bird, conjecturing on what wonderful rarity made that little noise can get you through the whole weekend. By far my favourite in this category is 'Possible Red-throated Pipit' (Red-throated Pipits are quite rare, and make a noise that is written down in the books as anything between 'Teeze' and 'Speee'). Lots of noises can be passed off as possible Red-throated Pipits: Red-wings, Skylarks, Tree Pipits, squeaky bicycles, mice. *And* just to make them a perfect mystery caller Red-throated Pipits are very rarely seen on the ground. Even *real* Red-throated Pipits tend to belt across calling a few times and disappear over the horizon.

Finally, I'd also like to add a word of thanks to the Wren which has a habit of keeping well out of sight in thick undergrowth and making little 'chacking' noises. These can inspire hours and hours of pulse-racing anticipation, as there are about 20 rare skulking warblers which also make little 'chacking' noises and hide in undergrowth.

So, that's the probables and possibles game. By all means play it and enjoy it. You can spend hours, days, even weeks, alone or with others chasing the *possible*. And even if (or rather *when*) it finally turns out to be the common species (which of course you *knew* it was all along) no-one will blame you. As long as you stick to the right species. Alas, some people do get a bit carried away and forget it's all a game and start promoting their possibles to probables, and then claiming them as 'definites'. This is how a lot of those stringy records get submitted to the rarities committee; and of course the rarities committee can spot them a mile off. The give-away is that the *same* common species are forever getting mis-claimed as the *same* rare species. You only have to look at the list of rejections in the *British Birds* 'Rare Birds' issue. Always the same ones – Albatrosses that were actually Gannets; American Ring-billed Gulls that were actually Common Gulls; lots and lots of American Waders that were only Dunlin; scores of Red-throated Pipits and Great Snipe (it's doubtful that Red-throated Pipits and Great Snipe exist at all); and county reports, pages full of rejected Red-breasted Flycatchers, which were clearly either Stonechats or Robins. So please, if you are going to send in duff gen, do the committee a favour and find something original!

Appendix 1 List of 1976 records not accepted

This list contains all the 1976 records not accepted after circulation to the committee. It does not include (a) those withdrawn by the observer(s) without circulation, after discussion with the honorary secretary; (b) those which, even if circulated, were not attributed by the observer(s) to any definite species; or (c) those mentioned in the monthly summaries in this journal, if full details were unobtainable. Birds considered to be escapes are also omitted.

Stilt Sandpiper	Chew Valley Lake, Avon, 20th April
Great Snipe	Near Fordingbridge, Hampshire, 28th January
	Cholderton, Andover, Hampshire, 13th February to 13th March
	Tresco, Scilly, 9th to 15th October
	Strumpshaw, Norfolk, 1st December
	Northam Burrows, Devon, 16th October
	Dowrog Common, St David's, Dyfed, 22nd October
Tawny Pipit	East Looe, Cornwall, 23rd to 27th January
	At sea, east of Sunderland, Tyne and Wear, 17th September
	Beachy Head, East Sussex, 19th September
Red-throated Pipit	Sandbach, Cheshire, 1st May
	Havergate Island, Suffolk, 2nd September
	Donna Nook, Lincolnshire, 24th to 25th September
	Chew Valley Lake, Avon, 4th October
	Porthgwarra, Cornwall, 17th October
	St Mary's, Scilly, 20th October
Citrine Wagtail	Belvide Reservoir, Staffordshire, ♀, 21st April
Black-headed Wagtail	Tresco, Scilly, 12th October

Remember this chapter was called 'Brightening up a dull day'? The possible-probables game is known to all birders and its appeal will never fade, nor its variations be exhausted. However, I have a new game for you. It's a bit mean, and I've never tried it out myself, but I think it could be fun, especially if you have the sort of warped sense of humour that enjoys practical jokes. I call this the ...

The first name game

It involves exploiting the over-enthusiasm of twitchers who are ravenous for a new tick. It is best played in the Isles of Scilly. I mentioned many pages ago that twitchers often abbreviate a bird's name, and some of these I find particularly irritating, though I'm not sure why. Maybe it's because it's somehow offensive to be so off-hand and chummy about a nice rare bird. A rare bird is rather special, and should be given a dignified title. I hate to hear an Icterine Warbler referred to as an 'Icky', or a Red-breasted Flycatcher as an 'RB flicker', or 'RB Fly' or even just an 'RB'. In the same way, twitchers tend to refer to rare birds only by the first word in the name, which is usually just an adjective. Hence a Red-throated Pipit becomes just a 'Red-throated', or the Red-breasted Flycatcher would be merely a 'Red-breasted'. The fact is that there are *other* and more common species that *share* the same adjective. For example, there is a *Red-throated* Diver and a *Red-breasted* Merganser. Neither of these is very rare, so if you are in Scilly and a twitcher asks anxiously, 'Where's the Red-throated?' he *assumes* that you know he means, 'Where's the Red-throated *Pipit?*' not, 'Where's the Red-throated *Diver?*' He's not interested in Red-throated Divers, because they're too common. So here comes the game, and it is *very naughty*. You seek out an anxious tick-hungry twitcher and wait for him to ask the inevitable 'Anything about?' To which you reply: 'Yes, over at such and such a place (make it some way away) I've just had a Red-throated,' and off he'll go, hoping to see a Red-throated Pipit! The one rule is, you *mustn't lie* – send him somewhere where you have *genuinely* seen a Red-throated Diver. Chances are, he won't even see the Diver, because Divers swim on the sea and Pipits don't (unless they are about to drown). Then try and find the twitcher again – you'll probably track him down by following the sound of his tears. You then complete the game by asking: 'Did you see it?' He'll reply, of course, 'No – where exactly was it?' And you finish him off: 'On the sea! Red-throated Diver.' Then just walk away and find another victim. He can't complain. You never told even the teeniest fib.

Here's a few suggestions you might care to try out if you want to play the first name game:—

'Have you seen the Spotted?' He'll assume Sandpiper or Crake, but it's actually Spotted Flycatcher or Red Shank or even Dick!

'Have you seen the Long-tailed?' He'll assume Skua or possibly Duck. It's actually Tit or Fieldmouse.

And here's a very good one, with lots and lots of misinterpretations:

'Have you seen the Lesser?' He'll assume Golden Plover, Kestrel, Grey Shrike, Yellow legs, or White-fronted Goose. It's actually a Black-backed Gull.

Tee hee! Isn't that naughty? And you can also play the game in reverse! Mention an adjective which is something fairly uncommon, but make it not *quite* rare enough for him to bother to go to see ... and then ... well, I'll give an example.

'Have you seen the Tawny?' He'll assume it's a Tawny Pipit, which is rare enough for you to mention but which he's almost certainly seen, because there are 20 or 30 recorded in Britain each year. In fact it's a Tawny Eagle, a first for Britain! So you also have the satisfaction of gripping him off too! Of course, you are less likely to get the chance to play this variation, as it does involve you finding a Tawny Eagle first. Come to think of it, if you have just found a Tawny Eagle you won't be bored enough to need to play any such wicked pranks on innocent twitchers. So, stick to the first version, and brighten up that dull day!

OK then, over the preceding chapters I have been through the process of what can happen when you find a rare bird or *think* you've found a rare bird, or desperately *need* to find a rare bird. It is the life-blood of birding. Some days you play your games and enjoy them; some days you make mistakes and admit it; other days you *don't* admit it; sometimes you deceive yourself, sometimes you might even deceive the committee; and sometime you'll be found out! But once in a blue moon you really *do* see a rare bird; you take your field notes; you send in your description; and your record is accepted – and there it is in *British Birds* for all to see. When the glory is so great no wonder men are sometimes corrupted in the search for it!

British Birds

VOLUME 70   NUMBER IO   OCTOBER 1977

Report on rare birds in Great Britain in 1976

John O'Sullivan and the Rarities Committee

This is the nineteenth annual report of the Rarities Committee. Details of the composition of the committee and other matters relating to its work during the year have already been published (*Brit. Birds* 70: 306-

suddenly the second, leading the September procession of Asiatic passerines.

Thrush Nightingale *Luscinia luscinia* (2, 26, 2)
Gwynedd Bardsey, immature, found dead, 20th September (K. Baker).
Shetland Out Skerries, 19th May (A. R. Lowe, W. E. Oddie). **I**
    (Scandinavia, east Europe and west Asia) The spring one continues the run of 18 spring occurrences since 1970. The September individual was the first for Wales and the most westerly ever.

Cetti's Warbler *Cettia cetti* (0, 254, 125)
Cornwall Skewjack, Porthgwarra, ♂, 4th April to 20th June (P. A. Maker, B. K. Mellow *et al.*). Porthgwarra, 13th November (W. R. Hirst, H. P. K. Robinson).
Devon Slapton Ley, present throughout the year, up to five singing in April, two to

7
Bird books

In my hurry to get to the scandalous bits, I have missed out an essential step in the process of bird identification – *looking it up in the book*. I have mentioned this several times, so *what book*?

The only bird book that is *truly* essential is a good *field guide*, full of nice accurate descriptions and pictures to help you figure out what you've seen. But in addition, there are literally hundreds and perhaps thousands of bird books in the shops. I would not for a second claim that the book you are now reading (which I presume is this one) is of any *practical* use at all. It's in pretty good company – *most* bird books aren't much use either! A lot of them are awfully nice to look at, but they are definitely not useful, and they may even be confusing. One of the most common categories of bird book is the kind that you are offered 'exclusively', through postal advertising. You know the routine – big white envelope, with plastic transparent panel, through which you can see what looks like a postal-order or a five pound note. '*Open this quickly. You Mr Oddie and you alone have already been awarded a prize which is your prize Mr Oddie, and nobody else's prize, but Mr Oddie's.*' The prize is in fact what you *thought* was a five pound note, but which is in fact only a bit of coloured paper, which tells you that you Mr Oddie

have been chosen for the opportunity of buying a big glossy
bird book, for a large amount of money which you could
buy at much the same exorbitant cost from your local
bookshop. If you *really* want it, it's quicker to go and buy
it from the shop; and you'll save hours and hours not sending
off vouchers, and you won't be lumbered with some lousy
bird print you don't like, *and* you'll avoid being chosen to
be sent books on flowers, and porcelain, and the Taj Mahal;
not to mention insurance deals and cheap holidays etc.

If you really want a big glossy bird book there's hundreds
of them, but it's not easy to tell one from the other, because
they're nearly *all* called *Birds of the World* or *The World of
Birds* or *Birds* or maybe, with disarming honesty, *A Book of
Birds*. (You can't complain to the Trade Descriptions Board
about that one!) One of the frequent drawbacks with these
books is that they turn out to have been printed in America
or Australia, and often contain not a single reference to anything ever seen in Britain. They are wonderfully random in
their coverage and tend to present birds in families rather than
species. You'll get pages and pages of Lorikeets and Trogons,
and not a single Bunting. This is because the *point* of these
books is to *look nice*. They are often quite good value, because
they are full of lovely colourful photographs and paintings,
but only of lovely colourful birds. I seriously suggest that
the best way to enjoy these books is to cut out the best pictures
and stick them all over your walls, or reorganise them into
one big scrap-book. No, *The World Encyclopaedia of Birds in
Colour* (Cockatoo Press, printed in Sydney) will *not* help you
to decide what that little grotty brown bird was you saw yesterday.

What you use for that is of course a *field-guide*. There are
quite a few books masquerading as field-guides – they are
usually called *British Birds*, or *Birds in Britain* (it seems there
is no copyright on bird-book names, so lots of them share
the same ones . . . confusing). There are also lots and lots of

books which just cover a certain selection of birds – *Birds of the Seashore* or *Birds in your Garden* (this no doubt means anybody else's garden too). These books tend to have the look of children's story-books (this is maybe because a lot of bird artists also illustrate children's story books). Of course, many of them are probably intended for kids; which is unfair on the kids who tend to take their hobby very seriously. I'm sorry if it seems as if I am implying that these books aren't serious, it's just that some of them are a bit daft! Their most common fault is that there doesn't seem to be much logic about which species are in the book and those which are left out. They ought really to be called not *British Birds*, but *Some British Birds* or *A Few British Birds*. To make them even more confusing they'll invariably include something as uncommon as a Spoonbill, because it looks weird and it's fun to draw, whilst leaving out say, a Rock Pipit, because it's a bit boring. A novice birder going to the sea-side armed with one of these books could be totally forgiven for getting pretty excited at finding a flock of Rock Pipits, which are so rare they aren't even in the book! But he'd be very disappointed that Blackpool beach isn't infested with Spoonbills!

Some of these books, again, are worth buying because the illustrations are so good; and some are worth buying because they are so *bad*; and they'll give you a good laugh if you know what the bird really looks like!

I honestly don't want to be mean. Any bird book is welcome but some are more welcome than others. Most welcome of all is a good *field-guide*. Fortunately, there are several *very* good field-guides, and all birders will be familiar with them and have their favourites. The most widely known (but I won't say the best because I'm trying to be impartial) are probably: *A Field-Guide to the Birds of Britain and Europe* (Peterson, Mountford and Hollam), *The Hamlyn Guide to Birds of Britain and Europe* (Bertel, Bruun and Arthur Singer) and *The Birds of Britain and Europe with North Africa and the*

Middle East (Heinzel, Fitter, Parslow). You will notice right away that Britain is getting bigger all the time. This is quite a dangerous tendency. Funnily enough, people don't often see a species if they don't know it exists. But start circulating pictures of new and wondrous species, and sooner or later somebody will start seeing them, especially if they are depicted in a book which is called *Birds of Britain and Europe*. It's fine to see a Tristram's Grackle or a Goliath Heron if you are in North Africa or the Middle East, but *not* on a reservoir outside Birmingham; and it's not even *very* likely in the Scilly Isles.

All these field-guides are excellent, and owning one of them is essential to birding in Britain. Mind you, they are not without flaws, and each guide has its own special flaw different from the others. Actually I suspect a conspiracy to make you buy all three (two of them are issued by the same publisher, so I bet *they* are up to something).

The Peterson field-guide arguably has the most immaculate illustrations, and an excellent system of little pointers indicating the most important identification features. On the other hand, it has the smallest selection of species (although it still covers most birds you are likely to see in Britain).

The Hamlyn guide has some nice little characterful sketches of birds in flight and on bushes, and in little silhouetted flocks, but to counteract this, in the illustrations, Mr Singer's birds seem to be rather misshapen, hunch-backed, pot-bellied and so on. No doubt a lot of these uncomfortable postures were necessary in order to squeeze so many species onto one little page; but they *do* look a bit arthritic. The Hamlyn guide also has a nasty system of relating the status of the bird to the whole of its world population rather than its frequency in Britain or Europe. Thus we get; 'Lanceolated Warbler – fairly common in dense vegetation of marshes, swamps and edges of lakes'. Fairly common in Thailand and Mongolia perhaps, but we are lucky if there's one a year in

Britain (and that almost invariably in Fair Isle), and it's hardly ever recorded anywhere else in Europe either! In fact there are little maps in the Hamlyn guide with little pink bits on showing the bird's range – if you look at the map for Lanceolated Warbler the little pink bit is *very tiny*, and somewhere in the middle of Russia! and *that's* where it's fairly common.

The Birds of Britain and Europe with North Africa and the Middle East doesn't make any dangerous statements about rarities and commonness – you just check it out on the maps, which are displayed for each species and are very good indeed. Actually, it's a very good book; but do remember it shows you all sorts of nice birds you *mustn't* start seeing in Britain! Mr Heinzel also gets high marks for showing birds facing in several different directions. Most field-guide illustrators have their birds all regimentally facing the same way, which is usually right to left. I sympathise, myself, as I am personally incapable of drawing a bird facing left to right. I have to turn the paper upside down or use a mirror. Just remember that birds are capable of facing in *all sorts* of directions; and they can fly, dangle, fall over, and even lie on their backs. I'm sure there must be some birders who depend so completely on their field-guides that they can't recognise anything unless it's facing right to left just like in the book.

If there is one final niggly criticism about field-guide illustrations, I suppose it would be that the nice easily-recognised males tend to get preference over the dowdy very-difficult-to-recognise (and even harder to paint) females and immatures, which are often depicted hiding behind the males. From what bits you can see peering out, they all look very much the same. Mind you they *do* look all very much the same!

My final words on field-guides are: *buy them*. As many as you can afford. Whilst I'm at it, I would like to put in a grateful word to the *Mitchell Beazley Bird-Watchers Pocket Guide*, which is tiny yet absolutely brimming with hundreds of cracking little paintings by Peter Hayman.

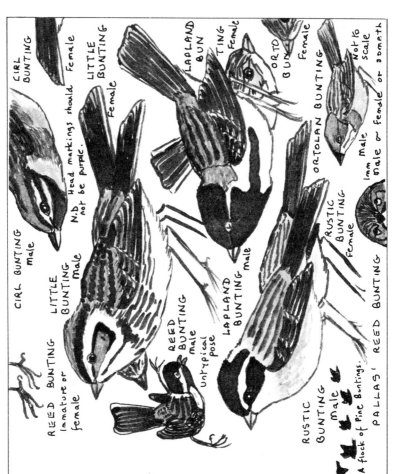

KEY TO MAPS

Pink area denotes breeding range. Red area denotes winter range. Blue area denotes migration route. Green area denotes area where the species has never been seen. Yellow area denotes the bits that aren't pink, red, blue or green.

LITTLE BUNTING
(Emberiza pusilla)

The smallest of all the Buntings. Extremely common in places where there are plenty of them. In areas where it is scarce the Little Bunting is not often seen. Easily confused with immature or female Reed Bunting (see illustrations for distinctions). By no means exclusively seen facing right to left. Call: an unmistakable 'tick' indistinguishable from a Robin

RUSTIC BUNTING
(Emberiza rustica)

Clearly larger than Little Bunting. Male easily distinguished. Female similar to Little Bunting; best identified by call – an unmistakable 'tick'.

NB: This map shows distribution of Yellow-breasted Bunting (see next page).

A field guide is essential to any birder. Which other books you consider to be essential depends on your particular involvement, special interests, or tastes. The most efficient way to check out what is available is to contact the Bird Bookshop (Scottish Ornithologist Club, 21, Regent Terrace, Edinburgh, EC7 5BT. Tel: 031 556 6042) and they'll not only send you a catalogue of just about every bird book currently available, but they'll also send you the actual books too – as long as you send them the money of course! And that, by the way, is a quite unsolicited recommendation. In fact all my recommendations are unsolicited. I just love bird books.

So, if I may end this chapter with a further recommendation, I do particularly enjoy the accounts by the nineteenth-century pioneer naturalists, who combined high adventure with their birding. Audubon's Journals, as he travelled across America, or Seebohm in Siberia, are all terrific stuff. I mean, we may think we take a few risks scrambling under the barbed wire when the farmer isn't looking, but these guys fought Indians, wrestled with buffaloes, fell down crevasses, got frozen alive in blocks of ice, and *still* kept ticking! And they didn't even have decent binoculars. Which is why they had to ... er ... 'collect' the bird sometimes. No room for sentiment, yet wonderfully romantic. If you have never read any of these, do try them. Here is an example of the style (extract from *The Birds of Alaska*):

Saturday 24th June: The ice on the river is now melting fast. This morning our guide was drowned for the third time this week. I count myself fortunate indeed only to have been drowned twice throughout the whole winter. I am finding it hard to keep going with no legs; but I have hopes that I may be able to trade some of my drawings for another pair when we reach the fur-trappers camp. The Meadow Larks are in full song. Pity it is that the Indians round these parts see fit to eat them so much. To me the

Meadow Lark tastes foul and unpalatable, and I much prefer the rancid beaver giblets which have become our staple diet. This afternoon I was obliged to disembowel six Indians who stood between me and the nest of a Buff-breasted Sandpiper. The bird was wonderfully well camouflaged, and my search for it was further hampered by the loss of my left eye, which was gouged out when I carelessly trod on a Grizzly Bear. Great, however, was my joy when I discovered the Sandpiper was already with four young in down. Truly the most enchanting creatures that I have ever set eyes upon, their little beaks were as delicate as porcupine quills and their plumage wonderously mottled with browns and yellows, with bellies as white as thistle-down. Their mother stood boldly, but a foot away, as I marvelled at her babes, which looked up at me showing no trace of fear. I shot them all.

Original illustration from *The Birds of Alaska*, 1872: Buff-breasted Sandpipers feigning injury ... [Oh, come on, they ain't feigning nothing!]

Oh it's not like that anymore ... It's so *easy* nowadays – bird clubs, field-guides, photos, tapes and records ... ah yes, tapes and records. Before we finally leave bird identification ... it's not too difficult to depict in a book what a bird *looks* like ... but it's damned near impossible to write down what it *sounds* like! So, on to ...

8
Bird noises

The problem seems to be that no two people hear the same noise (or bird-call) quite the same way; or rather, even if they do hear it in the same way, they don't write it down the same way. I recall when I did at last encounter the elusive Red-throated Pipit – which, true to the reputation of the species, was flying round calling and never once showed itself on the ground. It *was* a Red-throated Pipit though; honestly! How did we know? Because it *called* like a Red-throated Pipit. Well, there were four people there, and three of them had heard one before. *I* hadn't; but I *still* knew that what I was hearing was a Red-throated Pipit. Anyway, we decided to conduct a little experiment. We stood together and as soon as the bird called we all tried to describe what we heard.

Somebody said: 'It sounds a bit like a Redwing, but shorter and higher.'

Somebody else: 'It sounds more like a Tree Pipit, but much thinner.'

I decided to play safe and said: 'It sounds like a Red-throated Pipit' (which was really chicken ... no, it *didn't* sound like a chicken...).

So ... we listened again, and this time we all had a go at writing down the call. The four versions were 'Speee', 'Tseeze', 'Skee-er', and 'Pszeeee-az'; and just to add to the selection, the three field-guides have it down as 'Tseeh', 'tzeeaz', and 'skee-eaz'. So that's *seven* different versions for a start! It's in there *somewhere*. If you've heard a Red-throated Pipit, you'll get the general idea; but if you *haven't* heard a Red-throated Pipit, none of those versions will really tell you what it sounds like.

This is more or less what a Red-Throated Pipit looks like if you see one on the ground.
The lack of colour diminishes the whole effect somewhat but try and imagine the 'throated' bit is brick-red.
Wouldn't that look nice?
The little dot up above to the right is not a squashed fly - it is the usual view of a Red-throated Pipit. Try to imagine it going "spee" or "skeeaz" or "psseeeer" or if you've heard a real Red throated Pipit try to remember what it sounded like - ah happy memory!

The trouble is, there is no real substitute for hearing the real thing. Books try as best they can, but, just to balance up the seven different versions of the same thing, you can just as easily find the same thing for seven different species! For example, have a browse through the phonetic renderings in field guides and you'll find roughly a *dozen* different species that are supposed to go 'Pee-oo'. These include Little-ringed Plover, Pygmy Owl, Short-toed Lark, Wood Warbler, Ring Ouzel, Willow Tit and Snow Bunting – so that's seven different *families*, let alone species! You'll also find quite a few different birds that go 'Twik'; several that go 'tsip', and any amount that go 'chak'. The ones that are *really* frustrating say: 'identified by characteristic chak'! Exactly how that differs from the characteristic chak of about two dozen other species, you will only know when you've heard them all for yourself!

Actually, phonetics are rather fun. Some of them are a challenge to the tongue ... How *do* you pronounce: 'aahng-ung-ung' (Greylag Goose) or 'hihi heea' (Kite) or, here's a good one: 'tsissi-tseri-tsi, tsi, tsi, tsiu' (Hazel Hen) – I wonder if a Hazel Hen thinks of it that way?! And what *is* the difference between 'ki ki ki' (Merlin) and 'kee kee keee' (Kestrel)? Perhaps it's just a cheeky way of telling us they sound exactly the same. (But as a matter of fact, they don't.) By now you are possibly having a go at saying some of these out loud. There's hours of harmless fun here. (Another game to brighten up that dull day!) All right then, try Sooty Tern: 'kerwacky wack'. Silly eh? And how about trying a Caper-caillie – that's described as: 'a gutteral wretching call' (I've heard quite a few of those come to think of it) or, better still, have a go at the Capercaillie's song: 'beginning with "Tikup tikup tikup" and accelerating rapidly and ending with a "pop", like the withdrawing of a cork; and followed by a short phrase of "grating whispering notes"'. The whispering is probably from people thinking you've gone loony making silly noises. But there's no harm done – so you have a go.

Of course, if you want to cheat a bit and know what the birds really sound like, you might imagine that the best idea might be to buy records of them. Well, yes indeed, there *are* records of bird calls available, and some of them are very good. The abiding drawback, however, is that most of the birds on these records were recorded as they sat by their nests singing their little hearts out. Like the Yellow Hammer going: 'a-little-bit-of-bread and nooo cheese' (actually, you know, that description has never helped me much, as I have *never* heard a *person* say 'a-little-bit-of-bread and nooo cheese'). Anyway, like I said, the birds on record are usually full-plumaged males sitting in front of a microphone – in full song in the middle of summer. But the birds you can't recog-nise are grotty immatures belting over a hundred feet up in the air in autumn, and all they do is go: 'tsip' or 'chak' or 'pee-oo', or, in the case of the Yellow-Hammer – 'chip', 'twi-tick', 'tjip', 'twitup', 'twink' or 'twit' – depending on which book you read!

Like I said, you only *really* know them when you hear them. By all means refer back to the book to check out what you've heard, and indeed listen to those records too. It is well worth learning everything you can about what noises birds make, because it is not only an invaluable and necessary skill in bird identification, but you can sometimes also (and this is fun) lure the bird closer to you by imitating them. It is best to learn them from experience of course. You *could* try reading them from the book I suppose; but if you are discovered crouching under a bush going 'kerwacky wack' you'll probably embarrass yourself.

Another good way to embarrass yourself is to try 'pishing'. This is a technique introduced, I believe, by American birders; and it involves standing in woodland making little 'pish' noises. These are produced by kissing the back of your hand with tightly pursed lips. Honest, this is true. Go on, have a go. It tickles your lips doesn't it? Even if it doesn't lure birds, it's still a mildly pleasurable sensation, almost erotic indeed. In fact it often *does* lure birds. Apparently it works very well indeed on American Wood Warblers, in American woods. There aren't usually any American Warblers in English woods (unless you are very lucky), but pishing does seem to attract Fly-catchers and Titmice and several other species pretty well. *Why* it works, I'm not at all certain. I have heard a theory that the noise produced sounds like the squeak of a stoat or weasel, and that the birds come to chase it away. I doubt this. For a start, I think most birds, if they heard a weasel, would belt off in the opposite direction. Moreover, if the weasel theory were correct, they'd chase *me* away if I started 'pishing'; and I have *never* been chased away by Titmice! It may be that 'pish' sounds like the amplified 'swishing' of an insect's wings; hence the attraction for Flycatchers, hoping that you're going to turn out to be a giant midge. But I doubt this too. I prefer to think that birds have a sufficiently developed sense of humour to enjoy the spectacle of a human being hunched beneath a bush kissing the back of his hand. No wonder they come flocking to have a look. When they start going 'tsip' and 'chak', they are not answering back – they are falling about laughing! Fair enough. Birds give *me* a lot of pleasure – so if I can brighten up their day by doing a spot of 'pishing' for them, I'm happy to do so.

Yes, bird calls *are* a tricky area. There's no substitute for experience. It makes you grateful there's things like Curlews and Cuckoos that sound just like they ought to!

By the way, one final piece of advice from years of experience – if you hear a call and you don't recognise it – it's a Great Tit.

9
Where to look for birds

I have considered, then, many of the processes involved in identifying whatever it is you are seeing. How, though, can you improve your chances of finding something that *needs* identifying? If you are a full-time twitcher, you just sit by the phone and wait for news from the grapevine. But let's assume *you* want to get out and find something good for *yourself*. It is a matter of being at the right place at the right time. To a certain extent you might be able to anticipate the right place and the right time. So I will amend this chapter heading to...

Going to the right place

There are of course many nationally known good localities for watching birds and trying to find rare ones. In fact, there are so many of them that I'm not going to make any attempt to list them here. If you are a birder, you probably know more good places than I do. If you know any new ones please drop me a line. There are now two or three excellent ornithological equivalents to the *Good Food Guide*, most notably perhaps John Gooder's *Where to Watch Birds in Britain and Europe*. Like all birders I have certain places which I particularly enjoy visiting time and time again, but to write of all my experiences and travels would certainly take another book (and won't my publisher be pleased to hear that).

I suppose that most non-birders imagine that a large part of the appeal of bird-watching is that it gets you out in the country and takes you to all sorts of lovely places. Of course, as I presume this book has already demonstrated, this is a *very small* part of the appeal. It's a good thing it is only a small part, because many of the best bird localities are extremely ugly and unpleasant. Old fashioned sewage farms, with their open pans of festering excreta, attract wading birds, as well as flies and bird-watchers. To be honest, they are quite peaceful places, because no normal human being could put up with the stench without wearing a peg on his nose. Mind you, the peacefulness of one of the best sewage farms in Britain (Perry Oaks in Middlesex) is marred a *little* by the fact that it is almost in the middle of the main runway at Heathrow airport. It is one of the few places in Britain where you can be deafened and asphyxiated at the same time, while still watching a Temminck's Stint. Sewage outfalls on the coast are pretty good too; you can test your skill at distinguishing small rare immature gulls from large common mature floating turds. I'm not being gratuitously unpleasant – it's true!

Even some nationally famous bird-reserves are quite famously hideous. The bleak shingle waste-land of Dungeness, scattered with the skeletons of clapped-out fish-and-chip shops and glowered over by the monstrous atomic power station, must be one of the most godforsaken places on earth; but it's a great place for birds! Even the power station acts

as a lure, by pumping hot water into the sea which attracts
fish which attract rare terns and gulls; and they hover around
close enough to the shore for you to be able to identify them
properly! Portland Bill is one of my very favourite places
with a splendid bird-observatory, but I happen to know that
every night the warden prays that some knotted-hanky-
headed-day-tripper will drop a lighted cigarette and con-
flagrate the nastiest collection of holiday huts this side of
Butlins. And talking of Butlins, the holiday camp at Skeg-
ness has turned up a few rare birds in its time – no, honestly
it has; (no silly puns intended).

Of course there *are* some beautiful bird spots – the Scilly
Isles are gorgeous and Fair Isle is majestic. In fact, ironically,
the only thing that can spoil places like these is the number
of bird-watchers; but really there's plenty of room for us as
long as we behave. But everybody knows about Fair Isle and
Scilly, and Cley, and Minsmere, and all those. What is perhaps more interesting at this point is to consider briefly how
you can spot a *potential* good bird spot, closer to home as
it were. This is a matter of getting to know local habitats
and developing experience of which kind of birds tend to
occur habitually at certain kinds of places. And indeed certain
species *do* seem *so* exclusively attached to certain places that
there is hardly any point looking for them anywhere else.
It is common knowledge that Hoopoes are only *ever* seen on
vicars' lawns. Especially during September, you may well see
shabby-looking gentlemen peeping through knot-holes in
parsonage fences. They are not ecclesiastical peeping-toms,
nor are they engaged in out-door confessional – they are
birders looking for Hoopoes!

We noted earlier that most of the Red-breasted Flycatchers
reported were actually Robins or moulting Stonechats. You
can easily tell a *genuine* Red-breasted Flycatcher by the fact
that it is *only* visible when perched on a tangle of rusty barbed
wire at the bottom of a sea cliff. They very occasionally also

appear sitting on abandoned prams on beach rubbish dumps. You'll *never* see Stonechats or Robins on abandoned prams. Robins are invariably seen on the handles of garden-spades. The spade may be in a vicar's garden, so look out for Hoopoes too. But Stonechats *don't* appear in gardens or on spades. They *always* sit on gorse bushes, just like in the pictures in the books. In spring if you are looking for the first Wheatears, find a football pitch, because Wheatears love running up and down football pitches. Shrikes are only ever seen sitting on telegraph poles; and Buff-breasted Sandpipers are to be found trotting around on the airport on St Mary's in Scilly, and, as far as I know, they have never been seen anywhere else in the world. The books tell you that Buff-breasted Sandpipers are *supposed* to live in America, but I have been there lots of times and I have never come across one; and neither has any American birder I have ever met. It's honestly true that rich yankee twitchers charter trans-atlantic flights to Scilly, just to see a Buff-breasted Sandpiper!

It's a good thing birds *are* so loyal to their favourite places because birders do seem to have an almost touching faith that if a rarity once turned up at a certain spot, it's bound to happen again. I recall many years ago, when I was even smaller than I am now, a friend of mine declared that he was off to spend a day in early June at Selsey Bill, in Sussex. I asked: 'What do you hope to see?' He replied: 'Almost certainly a Great Reed Warbler.' I was impressed, and didn't question his confidence, not knowing at the time that it was based solely on the fact that a Great Reed Warbler had turned up at Selsey on the same date the previous year. As it happened, that Great Reed Warbler had been the first Great Reed Warbler *ever* seen at Selsey during years and years of solid coverage. The odds against another one turning up on the same date the following year must have made Selsey about the *last* place in Britain likely to get a Great Reed Warbler that June. My friend's faith was naive, but it really *should* have been rewarded – but it wasn't. Not only did he not see a Great Reed Warbler, he didn't see a single decent bird!

Mind you, the wondrous thing is that you sometimes *can* predict the appearance of a rare bird. My own most recent instance was when I was plodding the shoreline of the island of St Martin's in Scilly in mid-May. It was the first time I had ever been to St Martin's, so I had no idea of the favourite bird spots. I arrived at a patch of short-cropped grass and frivolously remarked to my companion, 'Mmmmm there ought to be a Tawny Pipit on here.' Within two seconds there was! That's no exaggeration. It literally leapt from behind a sand dune and landed right in front of us, as if I'd announced it at a Court Presentation. It was the only Tawny Pipit seen in Britain that spring – so what odds on that one?

Mind you, I'd had another clue. The thing I omitted to mention was that there was a strong east wind blowing that day. Bird-watchers are obsessed with the east wind, and to a point rightly so. The east wind blows from the Continent, and that's where many of the rare birds come from, including the Tawny Pipit. I know some birders who simply won't get out of bed unless the wind is from the east; but that's definitely an insult to the west, south and north winds, and all the other variations in between. All of these breezes are capable of wafting rare birds your way. So don't be silly about it. What's more, east winds can be totally useless, especially if it's a nice cloudless day and the birds are flying over several miles up.

Knowing which weather conditions are likely to produce good birds is of course a great skill that every birder should develop. I'm not going to go into all the complexities here, because other books have covered it ever so well. (I refer you to Ian Wallace's excellent *Discover Birds* – he's much more knowledgeable than I am and nothing like so frivolous.) However, I will pass on a couple of weather hints from my own experience which you may care to test out.

If you're into reservoir-watching, pray for *summer thunderstorms*. Before the storm, thunder clouds always seem to bring Black Terns – which are always nice to see. Beware though of Common Terns *looking* black, because the light is so awful. And after the thunderstorm, seek out those little marshy puddles – because you'll find it's rained Wood Sandpipers.

I must admit I'm very fond of rotten weather. Half-frozen reservoirs always seem to hold good wild fowl, and you get Lapwings and Golden Plovers flying over. And *fog* is terrific. You have to be wary in thick fog, mind you, because birds always look a lot *bigger*, especially on or near water. Common Gulls turn into Herring Gulls; Dab-chicks become rarer Grebes; ducks become geese; and, on inland reservoirs, the records of unidentified divers shoot up alarmingly. Fog does produce good migrant birds though, for the obvious reason that they are not daft enough to fly around in it crashing into one another, so they sensibly come into land until it lifts. It's a pity that it's usually too foggy to see them – not always though. My favourite fog story is from Fair Isle some years ago. The intrepid warden was blundering around the island in thick fog, determined to grip off the other timid birders who'd refused to leave the cosiness of the observatory and risk their lives falling over cliffs. Suddenly he spied another equally reckless explorer some way ahead of him. 'Anything about?' he yelled through the murk. There was no reply. He staggered a little closer. 'Seen anything?' he asked again. The silhouette didn't answer. It remained motionless – 'Obviously watching something good,' thought the warden, and edged closer still, creeping stealthily so as not to disturb whatever it was the engrossed figure was studying. He crept up to within whispering distance: 'What have you got, then?' At which point the figure turned round to face him – it was a Crane!

You see, fog *does* often produce good birds. It also produces lots of possibles and probables, which have usually disappeared when the fog lifts.

Early morning and dusk are widely considered the best *times* for seeing birds, and, again, there's a lot of truth in that. I confess myself to having an early morning obsession. I know some people find it hard to get up and get out, but not me. I find that, with no trouble at all, I can get up at six, I do without breakfast, get out into the field, enjoy half a dozen small cigars, and can be throwing up behind a hedge by eight o'clock. I'll be faint and delirious by half past; and back in bed at nine. And I've seen a lot of good birds that way. First light and late evening *are* the best birding times, and they are naturally also excellent for half seeing possibles and probables. Shadows and silhouettes all help to transform the common bird into a potential rarity. But you have to know when to give up. I have a rule. You know those pot things they have on the tops of telegraph poles? Well, when I start mistaking those for roosting Lesser Grey Shrikes, I know it's time to give up.

Identification of these three species should present no problem. They are of course, "Gorse", "Garden Spade" and "Rusty barbed wire"...

So go out to the likely looking places, at dawn, in thick fog, with an east wind, and you'll definitely have a good chance of seeing something interesting. There is one other way you can be led to a rare bird and I will call this chapter ...

10
Listening to the layman

It is one of the privileges (or penalties) of being a birder that
people are always coming up to you with reports of unfamiliar birds that they have seen. It's much the same for me being
a so-called comic; people are always telling me jokes. Most
of them are definitely not worth listening to, and it's the same
with these bird stories (but you can't always be *quite* sure).
A birder dreads the moment when somebody who definitely
isn't a birder comes and tells him: 'Hey, I've seen a funny
bird in my garden.' These funny bird sightings come from
all sorts of people, housewives, old ladies, chartered account-
ants, children, gardeners and, of course, vicars with lawns.
Of course you're lucky if a vicar tells you: 'I've seen this big
pink bird with black and white bits on it and a sort of a crest.'
That's a Hoopoe, and no mistake. *But* it's *not* a Hoopoe
because it's pink with black and white bits and a crest. It is
a Hoopoe because it's on a vicar's lawn.

If *anybody else* reports 'a big bird that is pink with black
and white bits and a sort of a crest', it's a Jay. In fact 99 per
cent of laymen's funny birds refer to Jays. Not that you'd
realise this from the descriptions you are given. It's extraordi-
nary how a Jay can be many things to many people. Here
are several different funny bird descriptions that I have personally been challenged to identify:

'It was a big bird with a long beak, entirely pink.'

'It was fairly small with a short beak; and bright blue.'

'It was medium-sized, and black and white. I didn't see the beak.'

'It had a white rump – that's all I saw – a white rump.'

They were *all* Jays. You have to assume this, or you'll go on a lot of wild Jay chases. And don't be distracted if the lay person appears to know a little bit about birds, unless of course he's a vicar. If a vicar says authoritatively: 'I've just seen a Jay on my lawn' – he's got it wrong – it was, of course, a Hoopoe. (Even vicars can cock it up.) Otherwise, you can be sure *any* pink, black, blue or white bird seen by a layman is a Jay. Even if they strenuously deny it, and even if they claim some bird-knowledge. It's amazing how stubborn these folks can be. You may well have a conversation like this:

'I've seen this funny bird in my garden. I wonder if you could tell me what it was?'

'It was a Jay.'

'Shall I describe it?'

'No. It was a Jay.'

'It wasn't a Jay.'

'Yes, it *was*.'

'No, it wasn't. I've seen Jays.'

'Yes I know, you saw one in your garden.'

'*This* one *wasn't* a Jay. Jays are black and white.'

'Yes, that's right.'

'This bird was pink and blue.'

'So are Jays.'

'You said they were black and white.'

'Jays are pink *and* black and white, *and* they have blue patches on the wings; and they've got white rumps.'

'Oh well in that case ... this *definitely* wasn't a Jay.'

At this point you calmly tear a field-guide out of the shelves and throw it at him. Don't just find a picture of a

Jay and ram it in his face. Be fair, and let him find it himself. Say to him: 'There's a book – pick it up. Go on, look at the pictures and tell me what you saw. Please.' But for God's sake don't give him *Birds of Britain and Europe with North Africa and the Middle East*. He'll turn straight to Sinai Rosefinch.

'That was *it*. Sinai Rosefinch.'

'No, it wasn't. That would be a first for Britain. Sinai Rosefinches live in the Sinai; *not* in your garden. *And* it wasn't a Red-fronted Serin either, *or* an Azure-winged Magpie, *or* a Bald Ibis. Have a look in *here*.' You now do what you should have done in the first place, you give him *The Observer's Book of Birds* (which only has common birds in it). He'll look through that and announce: 'It's not in here.'

Now, and only now, do you produce the biggest and best picture of a Jay you can find. It's worth getting one enlarged and framed. *Now* you shove it in his face.

'There, look at *that*.'

'That's a Jay.'

'Right. A Jay.'

'It *wasn't* a Jay.'

'Well it *wasn't* a Sinai Rosefinch.'

Of course you're *both* right. It was a Roller. Which would have been a tick if you hadn't wasted all that time arguing and had gone to see it.

The awful truth is, there are certain scarce birds that *only* show themselves to laymen. The Roller is one of them. Ordinary people seem to notice Rollers (not surprisingly because they are amazingly colourful and they do 'roll', which attracts attention) but birders *never* see Rollers; probably because they mistake them for Jays. In the same way, Waxwings are seen exclusively by housewives through their kitchen windows (always feeding on mountain ash berries – the Waxwings, not the housewives). It is worth following up reports on Waxwings because people know their name from seeing them on Christmas cards. Don't expect, though, just to amble up and tick them off. You may have to wash-up for several hours before they materialise. I'm convinced that Waxwings prefer being watched by housewives rather than birders; in the same way that rare ducks prefer being shot by wild fowlers; and rare birds of prey willingly risk being poisoned by gamekeepers rather than being stared at by harmless twitchers. So, if you *do* hear tell of funny birds, it's often not worth following up the reports, even if they sound reliable, because you probably won't see whatever it is.

O.K.— These three birds are Hoopoe, Jay and Roller, but not necessarily in that order. I'll leave it to you to sort them out. The colours involved are pink, black and white, with some bits of blue. This is a trick question — don't take too much notice of the 'observers'.... only ONE of them is a real vicar.

You are less likely to dip out on *small* birds, simply because I have never heard of a decent small rare bird being seen by a layman. If they tell you they've seen a funny *little* bird, it means it must have been highly-coloured, otherwise they wouldn't have noticed it. So it's almost certainly escaped from a cage – a Zebra Finch or an Orange-cheeked Waxbill or something. Or it might well be a male Chaffinch. The Chaffinch is actually the commonest bird in Britain, but it's amazing how many people say 'Well! I've never seen one of those before!'

If you want to know what a
male Chaffinch looks like,
turn back to the picture of a female
on page   and imagine it with
pretty colours : blue head, black & white
wings and pink underneath... and then
you'll realize you've seen thousands of them.

Zebra Finch, thinking of escaping.
Note how nature has developed
plumage camouflage ideally
suited to life in a cage.

11
Specialised pursuits

When all is said and done, no matter how much you know, and no matter who you listen to, the truth is more or less *any* bird can turn up, more or less *anywhere*. That is one of the most exciting things about birding – and one of the most exhausting. The possibilities and problems are endless. Little wonder then that some birders choose to limit themselves to certain specialist areas. I remember when I was birding in New York, I asked a local watcher for her advice on some of the small confusing little grey waders that occur on American shores. She replied, 'Oh I don't look at those anymore, they upset me.' They upset *me* too and I admired her solution. She seemed much happier for her decision. Neither had she copped out entirely: she didn't bother with those waders but she was 'into warblers' – which are just as confusing.

Maybe it's because other birds upset them that some birders choose only to look at raptors: others immerse themselves (sometimes literally) in counting wild-fowl. Or they become totally involved in trapping and ringing (some ringers would admit that they have lost the ability to identify any bird unless they are holding it in their hand), or you can get into bird photography; or drawing and painting birds; or you can devote a whole lifetime to the study of one particular species. By and large, I think specialists are happier and more relaxed than ordinary birders. They avoid a lot of the hassle and tension of twitching and chasing and dipping out and being gripped off. However, there is one specialist area that seems to combine every pitfall, discomfort and distress known to birders. And yet it seems it should be so *relaxing*. This activity is called...

Sea-watching

There are a few experts who, it seems, don't do much else *but* sea-watch, but *most* birders have had a go at it at some time or another. They would no doubt agree that sea-watching is *the* most tedious of all pursuits. Not just birdy pursuits. It easily beats the boredom of watching cricket, ladies tennis or 'Stars on Sunday'. It tends to be particularly unexciting, because a lot of birders only try sea-watching as a last resort, when there are no birds to be seen anywhere else. The same adverse weather conditions that produce nothing on the land produce nothing at sea either! So sea-watching is often just that. Watching the sea. Not sea *birds* – just *the sea*.

The *patience* of regular sea-watchers is legendary. They will lie there gazing at the waves for hours and hours and hours. Many of them settle down on the beach, with their telescopes on their knees, as the dawn rises, and they are still there at dusk. If you go and prod them they will often fall over, because they've actually been asleep most of the day. Some of them may be dead. The ones that stay alive and awake are either nervous wrecks or practiced stoics. If you sea-watch on your own, you will inevitably start to hallucinate, and stringing is rife. If any birds do ever fly past out to sea, they tend to belt across at break-neck speed at a vast distance from the shore. They will be visible for only a few seconds and they'll never be seen again. This being the case, the lone sea watcher can claim to have seen *anything* and no one can prove him wrong. So, if you do sea-watch by yourself, you'll have to put up with the fact that nobody will ever believe any of your records!

However, most sea-watching is done in groups. This way people can keep one another awake. On the other hand, the emotional strain is almost unbearable. The problem is that the field of view of telescopes and binoculars is so variable from one to another, and the vast expanse of ocean to be watched is so large, that it is most unlikely that any two people will be looking at the same bit of sea at the same time. Birders attempt to play fair by making rules to try to guarantee that everybody sees what few birds do belt past. So, everyone agrees to look at the *same* bit of water – straight ahead, say – about half a mile out and no one is allowed to pan left or right or up or down. They develop the skill of looking through their telescopes with one eye, whilst still keeping the other one open to see if anyone's cheating. An alternative system is for only *one* person to watch, and for everyone else to wait for him to see something. The problem arises if he *does* see something. He then has to tell everyone else which bit of sea the bird is flying over, and you've got about ten seconds before it has crossed the horizon and vanished for ever. It is agony, and it goes something like this dialogue between two seawatchers.

'Diver!'
'Where??'
'Flying west.'
'Which is west?'
'Right.'
'So it's flying left to right?'
'Yes.'
'How far out?'
'I daren't take my telescope off it.'
'Try to pin-point it.'
'Can you see the boat?'
'There's hundreds of boats!'

'A red boat.'
'Yes. A big red boat?'
'No. A little red boat.'
'A little red boat, with a green sail?'
'Yes.'
'I've got that.'
'Well it's gone past that.'
'How far past?'
'Have you still got the boat?'
'The little red one?'
'With a green sail?'
'Yes.'
'OK, come past that ... keep going right and you'll see a kittiwake.'
'On the water, or flying?'
'On the water.'
'There's fifty kittiwakes on the water!'
'OK, second kittiwake from the left.'
'That's a Common Gull.'
'No; next to the Common Gull.'
'OK. I've got it. A Kittiwake, next to a Common Gull.'
'Right, now, go eleven o'clock from that, and you'll see a buoy.'
'I can't see a buoy.'
'Eleven o'clock from the kittiwake. A small boy – swimming.'
'That's not a boy. It's a girl!'
'Oh yes. And she's not swimming. She's drowning!'
'Never mind that, have you got her?'
'Yes.'
'Right then. Count one ... two, three ... er ... ten, eleven ... twelve ... twenty-five, twenty-six, twenty-seven ... er, er ... thirty-three, thirty-four, thirty-five waves to the right, and there's a bit of drift wood, with a Great Northern Diver flying over it ... Now!'

'Er ... I've got the boat!'

It is a real test of a seawatcher's skill to be able to identify birds rollicking over waves way out in the distance. But some of the claims are truly outrageous. The confident expert will pick out dots beyond the range of normal human vision and tick them off as rare Petrels or Shearwaters. It is very intimidating to be sitting next to one of these guys, who seem to

'Captured' in the telescope for all to sea !
Great Northern Diver, Bulwer's Petrel
and Wasp.

have sight like Superman and keep yelling out the names of rare birds you've hardly ever heard of, let alone seen. Fortunately there is usually only *one* of these people in any group, so if the rest of you club together you can soon brand him as a stringer. Mind you, you'll never quite get over the nagging doubt that what you'd reckoned was a migrant wasp fifty yards out, really *was* in fact a Bulwers Petrel six miles out, just like *he* said it was. The most modest approach to sea-watching is to put a false limit on the extent of your

vision, and focus *only* on a manageable area, between half
a mile and a mile away. You'll still miss stuff though, as you
are looking *over the top* of those birds flying along the shoreline, right in front of your eyes!

Sea-watching can be *so* frustrating, that it is no wonder
that many perverse birders succumb to the all-too-easy
temptation of gripping people off as they sit together on the
shoreline in nervous little packs. It is so *easy*; and it is wickedly
satisfying to be able to upset people who are literally sitting
next to you. Inexperienced sea-watchers are so unsure of their
ability to identify anything out at sea that they usually don't
risk pronouncing judgement until the bird is well out of
sight. What you have to do is *get in first*. You've got to time
it. Everybody has been staring silently through their telescopes and nobody has said a word for several minutes. Suddenly you lie back and look pensive for a moment. Then you
ask: 'Well ... what did you make of *that* then?'

This will be greeted with an indignant chorus of, 'What
did we make of *what*?!'

'That albatross.'

'*What* albatross?'

You then feign remorse: 'Oh I'm *sorry*! I assumed you
were all looking at it! About five miles out. Didn't *anyone*
see it?'

There won't be a reply. They'll either have fainted, or leapt
into the sea to end it all. Take no notice – just busy yourself
scribbling notes and doing little sketches, whilst muttering:
'Possible Black-browed'. Of course you've no intention of
submitting the record to the rarities committee, but you'll
seem *ever so* virtuous when you announce: 'I shan't send it
it – 'cos I can't be *quite* sure.' The others will probably forgive
you (if they haven't already drowned themselves), and there's
no harm done and nobody missed out on anything; because
it was really only an immature Gannet!

Seawatching is, I'm sure, excellent character training. If

you can truly learn to deal with the disappointments, deceits and disciplines you will have achieved a philosophical fatalism that Sophocles would have envied. If nothing else, you'll become dead accurate at throwing pebbles at tin cans.

12
On being a bird person

Over the past pages I have covered a lot of aspects of birding – the joys and the heartbreaks! So have I put you off or not? Are you going to become a birder or even a twitcher or maybe a dude? If you are already into birds I have no doubt you will have been treating my glib cynical facetiousness with the derision it deserves; but I do hope you've enjoyed it.

In the long-run, birders must *stick together*, whatever we care to call ourselves or call one another. We will always be the butt of easy ridicule. It's unavoidable. You only have to start talking birds in public and people will laugh at you. You can't blame them. Be honest, birds often have very *silly* names – Bar-tailed Godwit! Short-toed Tree Creeper! They do sound a bit daft don't they? (Mind you, if you think *they* are embarrassing just have a bit of sympathy for American birders. They have to talk about Yellow-bellied Sap-Suckers, and Blue-faced Boobies!)

We also have to endure endless witless bird jokes. It's amazing how apparently sophisticated people, who ought to know better, are unable to resist such facile jibes as:

'Oh you like birds, eh? The two legged kind, eh, eh?'

You should then wearily point out that *all* birds have two legs (unless they're crippled). That'll make them feel uncomfortable about reminding you of crippled birds. And the next time someone says: 'I'm a bit of a bird-watcher myself, know what I mean?' you say: 'No, I *don't* know what you mean. Do *please* explain; slowly please, and preferably with slides and diagrams.' Really make them *suffer*. Make them examine *why* they have just come out with a so-called 'joke' that is not only cheap, vulgar and sexist, but also *very very old*.

OK, serious bit coming up . . . Certainly there are factions in the bird world, but we must all ultimately unite and declare our common interest. There is no better and more practical gesture than joining the Royal Society for the Protection of Birds. The RSPB has perhaps got something of a dude image. It is certainly true that the RSPB gift catalogues seem to cater as much for the collectors of silverware, porcelain and Christmas cards as for the bird watcher. Certainly a portion of RSPB funds are derived from the dying bequests of wealthy landed gentry. It is also true that when I complained to an RSPB council member that the annual general meeting had been fixed for 18 October – right in the middle of the peak migration period! – he replied that it didn't matter too much because not that many council members were bird-watchers! It's just as well, because the work of the RSPB staff is never-ending. They don't have much *time* to get out birding. Make no mistake though, every penny of RSPB funds goes *exactly* where it belongs – *to the birds*. There is not a birder in this country who does not benefit directly from RSPB activities. Nearly every good bird area in the country is under some kind of RSPB conservation; and as more land, water and marshes get swallowed up by development and pollution, this protection is more and more necessary. Without the continued influence and involvement of societies like the RSPB, not only would the quality of birding diminish, but so would the quality of life itself.

Any birder who is not already a member should have his binoculars confiscated! So join now ... please. That was the serious bit, and boy, *do I mean it!*

It's all too easy to send up some aspects of RSPB advertising, so I will ... not that this is in any way, meant to resemble a page from *Birds* magazine.

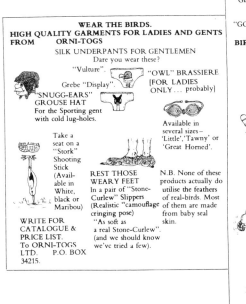

WEAR THE BIRDS.
HIGH QUALITY GARMENTS FOR LADIES AND GENTS
FROM   ORNI-TOGS

SILK UNDERPANTS FOR GENTLEMEN
Dare you wear these?

"Vulture".

Grebe "Display".   "OWL" BRASSIERE
                                     [FOR LADIES
"SNUGG-EARS"   ONLY ... probably]
GROUSE HAT
For the Sporting gent
with cold lug-holes.

Available in
several sizes –
'Little','Tawny' or
'Great Horned'.

Take a
seat on a
"Stork"
Shooting
Stick
(Avail-   REST THOSE   N.B. None of these
able in   WEARY FEET   products actually do
White,   In a pair of "Stone- utilise the feathers
black or   Curlew" Slippers   of real-birds. Most
Maribou)   (Realistic "camouflage of them are made
               cringing pose)   from baby seal
WRITE FOR   "As soft as   skin.
CATALOGUE &   a real Stone-Curlew".
PRICE LIST.   (and we should know
To ORNI-TOGS   we've tried a few).
LTD.   P.O. BOX
34215.

FEED YOUR FEATHERED FRIENDS
WILD BIRD FOOD
"GLIDE" – Bread crumbs, bits of old potato peel,
           shredded worms and squashed flies. Ideal for
           Tits, sparrows & Robins. 50p per packet.
"GOBBLE" – Tits, Sparrows and Robins. Ideal for owls
           and hawks. £2·15 per packet.
BIRD TABLES   "NATURAL".
           Lies on the ground. Looks just like
           a piece of wood.
           £4·75.

           "CHIPPENDALE"
           Genuine antique. Woodpeckers love them.
           £6,005. 25 + V.A.T.

BIRD CHAIRS: **HEATED BIRD-BATH**
ALUMINIUM,
COLLAPSIBLE.
Birds are not in fact
sitting on chairs –   This bath will hold up to
but you will enjoy   17 Greenfinches at a time.
hours of merry   It is made of white or pink
laughter watching   porcelain, and comes with
them try, especially   a non-slip rubber bath mat
when the chair   and two cakes of scented
collapses. £2·10.   soap (loofahs extra).
THE "TEE-HEE"   In cold weather the thermostat
TIT FEEDER   automatically switches on the gas
See the little tits   flames beneath – thus heating the
trying to get at their bath water, A real joy to the
food, dangling upside birds when they are cold and
down for hours till   hungry.
the blood rushes to   [Or if you are cold and hungry –
their heads and they   set the thermostat to, 'boiling' and
fall off. £3·50.   within seconds – hey presto! –
                       nourishing Greenfinch Soup]

BIRD CUSHION
For soft landing,   **OR WHY NOT**
when the little Tits   **GO THE "HOLE" WAY?**
fall off.   GIVE A HOME TO THE BIRDS
(Stuffed with real   – YOUR HOME.
Wren feathers).£5·15.   Buy one of our
                            custom made
                            FRONT
NEST BOXES Small size – suitable   DOORS with a
                for Titmice etc £1·50. Blue Tit size
                Large size – suitable   hole already in
                for Vultures,   it. In no time
                Ostriches or 12   at all your   And you can £85·00
                Pakistanis. £120·05.   house will   move into
                                        be infested   one of our
ALL AVAILABLE FROM   with happy Large size nesting boxes.
TWEETI-PRODS,   little tits!
"The Nest", Tweeville, HERTS.

and why NOT SAVE THEM THE TROUBLE?
Buy a bag of COMFI-NEST
nesting material (feathers, confetti,
sawdust & wool) and instruction
book "HOW TO BUILD A
BLUE TIT'S NEST". *You* build
£0·75p. £2·00   their nests whilst THEY have a
nice lie-down on a ...

"COZI-TIT"   £3·90.
"lounging couch"

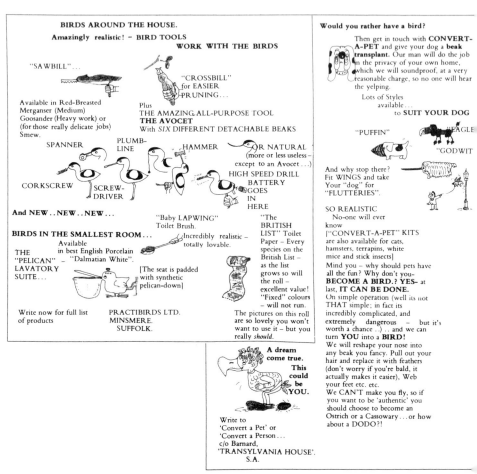

BIRDS AROUND THE HOUSE.

Amazingly realistic! – BIRD TOOLS

WORK WITH THE BIRDS

"SAWBILL"...

Available in Red-Breasted Merganser (Medium) Goosander (Heavy work) or (for those really delicate jobs) Smew.

"CROSSBILL" for EASIER PRUNING...

Plus
THE AMAZING ALL-PURPOSE TOOL
THE AVOCET
With *SIX* DIFFERENT DETACHABLE BEAKS

SPANNER   PLUMB-LINE   HAMMER   OR NATURAL (more or less useless – except to an Avocet...)

CORKSCREW   SCREW-DRIVER

HIGH SPEED DRILL
BATTERY
GOES
IN
HERE

And NEW..NEW..NEW...

"Baby LAPWING" Toilet Brush.
Incredibly realistic – totally lovable.

BIRDS IN THE SMALLEST ROOM...

THE "PELICAN" – LAVATORY SUITE...

Available in best English Porcelain – "Dalmatian White".

[The seat is padded with synthetic pelican-down]

Write now for full list of products

PRACTIBIRDS LTD.
MINSMERE.
SUFFOLK.

"The BRITISH LIST" Toilet Paper – Every species on the British List – as the list grows so will the roll – excellent value! "Fixed" colours – will not run. The pictures on this roll are so lovely you won't want to use it – but you really *should*.

Would you rather have a bird?

Then get in touch with **CONVERT-A-PET** and give your dog a **beak transplant.** Our man will do the job in the privacy of your own home, which we will soundproof, at a very reasonable charge, so no one will hear the yelping.

Lots of Styles available...
to **SUIT YOUR DOG**

"PUFFIN"   EAGLE
"GODWIT"

And why stop there? Fit WINGS and take Your "dog" for "FLUTTERIES".

SO REALISTIC
No-one will ever know
["CONVERT-A-PET" KITS are also available for cats, hamsters, terrapins, white mice and stick insects]
Mind you – why should pets have all the fun? Why don't you- **BECOME A BIRD.? YES-** at last, **IT CAN BE DONE.**
On simple operation (well its not THAT simple; in fact its incredibly complicated, and extremely dangerous – but it's worth a chance ..) .. and we can turn **YOU** into a **BIRD!**
We will reshape your nose into any beak you fancy. Pull out your hair and replace it with feathers (don't worry if you're bald, it actually makes it easier), Web your feet etc. etc.
We CAN'T make you fly, so if you want to be 'authentic' you should choose to become an Ostrich or a Cassowary...or how about a DODO?!

A dream come true. This could be YOU.

Write to 'Convert a Pet' or 'Convert a Person... c/o Barnard, 'TRANSYLVANIA HOUSE'. S.A.

OK, since we're now in a silly mood let's stay that way. I know many birders love to sing. A little merry singing can while away those tedious hours when there are no decent birds to look at – admittedly *too much* singing can scare away everything in sight! Nevertheless, I shall conclude with a few ornithological ditties. Console yourself when you've dipped out or celebrate when you've had a tick, or just sing to proclaim the sheer joy of birding. Or you needn't sing at all if you don't want to. I don't really care. I'm *still* going to conclude with a selection from...

13

The birder's songbook

Just to prove that these bird shanties have a long tradition, I'll start with one written at Cley way back in 1961. This was sung heartily as we trudged down Blakeney Point.

(To be sung to the tune of *Seventy-six Trombones*)

Seventy-six Greenshanks led the big parade,
With a hundred and five Godwits close behind,
They were followed by rows and rows of Hirundines
    and crows
And gulls of every shape and size.

Seventy-six Greenshanks marched along the beach,
With a hundred and five Godwits, strange to tell
There were literally files and files of mainly juveniles
And even downy young as well.

> There were *laridae* and *scollopacidea*,
> Dabbling, paddling, all along the shore,
> Pratincoles and Black-winged Stilts,
> That went in right up to their hilts
> And came out much wetter than before

There were Greylag Geese and Whooper Swans and Barnacles
Squabbling, wobbling all along the lake.

And if you take a closer look, you're sure to see a
  Long-tailed Duck
Looking for a Long-tailed Drake.

Seventy-six Greenshanks waited on The Point,
For One hundred and five Godwits to appear,
They were followed by ranks and ranks of Greater
  Yellowshanks,
With a big bad Bonxie at the rear.

The species mentioned were of course pure fantasy. It was
one of the most tedious holidays I have ever known! Hence
the need to alleviate the boredom by making up silly songs.
Bringing us right up to date, this one was written in Thailand
while studying Phylloscopus Warblers. It was inspired by
spotting a Thai farmer who bore a striking resemblance to
George Formby! *He* was a tick but the bird we were watching wasn't.

When I'm watching warblers (to the tune of *When I'm cleaning
windows*)
(after ukelele introduction)

> Hey, there's a warbler in a tree
> I wonder what it's going to be
> It looks like Pallas's to me
> When I'm watching warblers.
>
> A great big supersilium
> White and silky on its tum
> I bet it's got a yellow bum
> When I'm watching warblers.
>
> It's got a double wing bar
> But now I've seen its rump
> It's greenish-olive like its back
> Oh heck I feel a chump.

By now I've gathered quite a crowd
I wish I hadn't spoken so loud
It's just a bleedin' Yellow-browed
When I'm watching warblers

And here is a bird song about bird-song:

(To the tune of *British Grenadiers*)

Some talk of Capercaillies and some of Nightingales
Some love the 'chak' of Wheatears, or the
     'quick-quick-quick' of Quails
But of all the British bird-calls
There's none that can compare
With the 'tswee wee wee wee wee wee weeee'
Of the Common Sandpip – er.

Or this short lament:

(To the tune of *I tawt I taw a puddy tat*)

I tawt I taw a Spotted Crake
Creeping down a drain.
Oh no! It's just a Water Rail
And I've dipped out again!

OK, so now that you've got the idea, if you've really got
nothing better to do, how about making up a few yourself?
Just to start you off, may I suggest a few potentially fruitful
ornithologically appropriate titles? For twitchers, 'Let's
Twitch Again – like we did last autumn'. Or how about
'Stringing in the Rain' or indeed 'Hey Dude'? Or, if you
don't fancy writing your own, you can stick to one of the
many birding shanties that already exist. 'Thank Heavens for
little Gulls', 'Loon River' and of course Rolf Harris's famous
birding-hit 'Ptarmigan-garoo Down Sport'.

Recommended book list

My definition for this recommended book list is books about British birds that I own and find myself reading and actually *using*. I've got lots of lovely bird books that are ever so good but that I hardly ever look at. This is, by the way, a perfectly serious and, I hope, helpful list, not at all satirical or sarcastic.

Identification

FIELD-GUIDES

A Field Guide to the Birds of Britain and Europe – Peterson, Mountford and Hollom (Collins, 1976).
The Birds of Britain and Europe, with North Africa and the Middle East – Heinzel, Fitter and Parslow (Collins, 1977).
The Mitchell Beazley Bird-watchers Pocket Guide – P. Hayman (Mitchell Beazley, 1979).
British Birds: A Field Guide – A. J. Richards (David & Charles, 1979).

SPECIALIST IDENTIFICATION

Flight Identification of European Raptors – Porter, Willis, Christensen and Neilsen (Poyser, 1976).
Identification and Aging of Holarctic Waders (BTO Guide No. 17).

Williamson's Warbler Guides (BTO Guides 1, 2, 3).
Frontiers of Bird Identification – J. T. R. Sharrock (To be published 1980).

GREAT BIG BOOKS

The *Handbook of British Birds* (five volumes published by Witherby but out of print) which is awfully good but will, if we live long enough to see it, be superseded by *Birds of the Western Palearctic* (RSPB 1978–9), which has only two volumes out as yet, but we really should try to stay alive to see the rest because it's very good.

WHERE TO WATCH BIRDS

Where to watch birds – J. Gooders (André Deutsch, 1975).
Bird Observatories in Britain and Ireland (Poyser, 1976).

THINGS FOR BROWSING THROUGH AND ANTICIPATING WHAT YOU MIGHT SEE IF YOU EVER GO TO THE VARIOUS PLACES

All annual reports of bird observatories and county bird clubs. If you are considering visiting a particular area, I really do recommend having a browse through the relevant reports. It will help you figure out the best time of year for your visit and give you some detailed knowledge of local place names and so on. Also have an envious look at *Rare Birds in Britain and Ireland* by J. T. R. and E. M. Sharrock (Poyser, 1976).

ESSENTIAL MONTHLY READING

British Birds. The bird magazine. Don't borrow or pinch one, order your own. It's not expensive, considering the terrific value. In the same way that everyone should be a member of the RSPB, any birder should be chastised and punished who does not take *British Birds*. It's a long-term investment too; I have a full set of issues dating back to 1956 and I constantly find myself referring to identification papers, photographs, etc. etc. from years ago.

Otherwise I am, in fact, an avid non-reader (I was put off by studying English literature at university). Years and years have passed without my reading a proper book from cover to cover (I even had trouble checking the proofs of this one!) and yet I *always* read *British Birds* each month, every page of it, so it *must* be good. Order from Macmillan Journals Ltd, Brunel Road, Basingstoke, Hampshire RG21 2XS. You'll never regret it.

HOW TO DO IT

Discover Birds – D. I. M. Wallace (Whizzard Press/André Deutsch, 1979). Enthusiasm; expertise and terrific illustrations in one little volume. The perfect antidote to *Bill Oddie's Little Black Bird Book* (Eyre Methuen, 1980).

ADVENTURE, ROMANCE, DANGER ... AND BIRDS

Birds of Siberia – Seebohm (A. J. Sutton, 1976)
Audubon and his Journals (2 vols, Dover Publications, New York, 1960).

SOMETHING NICE TO LOOK AT

A Sketch Book of Birds – C. Tunnicliffe (Gollancz, 1979).

And don't forget – lots and lots of books, guides, pamphlets, magazines, (and membership forms) etc. are published by the RSPB on all possible aspects of birds and birding. Enquiries to: RSPB, The Lodge, Sandy, Beds. And remember, for any and all the bird books (even this one), try the Bird Bookshop, Scottish Ornithologists Club, in Edinburgh (see p. 110).

And, honestly, nobody has paid me for the plugs – if you don't believe me, ask them!

Finally, thanks to all birders, and birds, for making this book possible. You've got a lot to answer for! 'Ta.

Bill Oddie, 1980

The End